IN PERFORMANCE

IN PERFORMANCE

Contemporary Monologues for Teens

JV Mercanti

Applause Theatre & Cinema Books
An Imprint of Hal Leonard Corporation

Published in 2015 by Applause Theatre & Cinema Books
An Imprint of Hal Leonard Corporation
7777 West Bluemound Road
Milwaukee, WI 53213

Trade Book Division Editorial Offices
33 Plymouth St., Montclair, NJ 07042

Permissions can be found on page 263, which constitutes an extension of this copyright page.

Printed in the United States of America

Book design by Mark Lerner
Composition by UB Communications

Library of Congress Cataloging-in-Publication Data
In performance : contemporary monologues for teens / [edited by] J V Mercanti.
     pages cm
 ISBN 978-1-4803-9661-6 (pbk.)
 1. Monologues—Juvenile literature. 2. Acting—Auditions—Juvenile literature.
 I. Mercanti, J. V., editor.
 PN2080.I522525 2015
 808.82'45—dc23

                            2015016073

www.applausebooks.com

CONTENTS

Preface   xiii

Introduction   1
Etiquette for Scene Study, Rehearsal, and Beyond   27

MEN'S MONOLOGUES

A Hard Rain   33
by Jon Bradfield and Martin Hooper

Sondra   36
by Laura Cahill

The Day I Stood Still   40
by Kevin Elyot

Burnt Orange   44
by Lila Feinberg

Baby Girl   48
by Edith Freni

How We Got On   52
by Idris Goodwin

How We Got On   56
by Idris Goodwin

How We Got On   60
by Idris Goodwin

The Tutor   64
by Allan Havis

The Tutor   68
by Allan Havis

The Greatest Show on Earth   72
by Michael Kimmel

Henry's Law   76
by Stacie Lents

Snow Angel   80
by David Lindsay-Abaire

Peddling   84
by Harry Melling

Apocalypse Apartments   89
by Allison Moore

Apocalypse Apartments   92
by Allison Moore

girl.   95
by Megan Mostyn-Brown

The Connector   99
by Tim Murray

Madame Melville   103
by Richard Nelson

Edith Can Shoot Things and Hit Them   107
by A. Rey Pamatmat

Edith Can Shoot Things and Hit Them   111
by A. Rey Pamatmat

Edith Can Shoot Things and Hit Them   115
by A. Rey Pamatmat

Edith Can Shoot Things and Hit Them   119
by A. Rey Pamatmat

Lessons from an Abandoned Work   123
by Mona Pirnot

3:59AM: a drag race for two actors   127
by Marco Ramirez

Four   131
by Christopher Shinn

Four   135
by Christopher Shinn

The Curious Incident of the Dog in the Night-Time   139
by Simon Stephens

Exit Exam   143
by Mara Wilson

WOMEN'S MONOLOGUES

Dig Dig Dig   149
by Nikole Beckwith

Untitled Matriarch Play (Or Seven Sisters)   153
by Nikole Beckwith

Great Falls   157
by Lee Blessing

Sondra   161
by Laura Cahill

Perched   165
by Lila Feinberg

Burnt Orange   169
by Lila Feinberg

Baby Girl   173
by Edith Freni

Cutting   177
by Kathleen Germann

How We Got On   180
by Idris Goodwin

Strike-Slip   184
by Naomi Iizuka

Appropriate   188
by Branden Jacobs-Jenkins

Don't Talk, Don't See   192
by Julie Jensen

Chronicles Simpkins Will Cut Your Ass   195
by Rolin Jones

Unlikely Jihadist   198
by Michael Kimmel

Henry's Law   202
by Stacie Lents

All Hail Hurricane Gordo   206
by Carly Mensch

girl.   210
by Megan Mostyn-Brown

girl.   214
by Megan Mostyn-Brown

Franny's Way   218
by Richard Nelson

Franny's Way   222
by Richard Nelson

Edith Can Shoot Things and Hit Them   226
by A. Rey Pamatmat

Edith Can Shoot Things and Hit Them   230
by A. Rey Pamatmat

Playing with Grown Ups   234
by Hannah Patterson

Lessons from an Abandoned Work   238
by Mona Pirnot

Lessons from an Abandoned Work   242
by Mona Pirnot

A Numbers Game   246
by Tanya Saracho

Port   249
by Simon Stephens

Ancient Gods of the Backwoods   253
by Kathryn Walat

Exit Exam   257
by Mara Wilson

Acknowledgments   261
Play Sources and Acknowledgments   263

PREFACE

One of the best auditions I've ever seen was for Roundabout Theatre Company's 2001 revival of Stephen Sondheim and James Goldman's musical *Follies*. Jim Carnahan, the casting director, and I had called in Judith Ivey for the role of Sally Durant Plummer. If you don't know who Judith Ivey is, please Google her immediately. You have most likely seen her in something on stage, in film, or on television. You might also have seen a production that she's directed. She is a prolific artist.

The role of Sally Durant Plummer is fragile and complex. Sally has been married to Buddy for years, but all that time she has been pining for the love of Ben Stone, who is (unhappily) married to Sally's former best friend, Phyllis. Sally is going crazy with love and desire that has been burning for over twenty years.

Ms. Ivey was asked to prepare a cut from Sally's famous first-act song "In Buddy's Eyes," an aria through which she tries to convince Ben, in order to make him jealous, that she's deliriously happy in her life with Buddy. She was also asked to prepare a short scene from the show. Present in the room for the audition were Stephen Sondheim, the composer and lyricist; Matthew Warchus, the director; Todd Haimes, artistic director; Jim Carnahan, casting director; Paul Ford, the accompanist; a reader; and myself.

Walking into the room as herself, Ms. Ivey conversed with Mr. Warchus and Mr. Sondheim about her career and, very briefly, about the character. She then took a moment with Paul Ford to discuss the music. Following that, she came to the center of the playing space, closed her eyes, took a deep breath, and prepared herself to begin acting. In that moment of preparation, which truly lasted no longer than a breath, her body changed, her physicality changed, the very air around her seemed to change. She took the character into her body. Ms. Ivey then opened her eyes, nodded at Mr. Ford, and began to sing.

Ms. Ivey executed the song with specificity, a rich but contained emotional connection to the material, a strong objective, carefully thought-out actions, and a deep understanding of this woman and her desire. She went directly from the song to the scene, completely off-book (lines memorized), and when she finished—the room was silent. Mr. Sondheim had tears in his eyes. Mr. Warchus didn't have a word of direction to give her. It was not that Ms. Ivey had provided us with a complete performance. No, not at all. She had shown us the possibility of what she could create. She had shown us the potential of her Sally Durant Plummer. Her point of view was clear, consistent, and deeply, deeply affecting.

"Thank you, Judith. That was wonderful," Matthew Warchus finally said.

"I really love Sally," she responded, "But I was wondering if you might also consider me for the role of Phyllis. I've prepared that material as well."

"Of course I would. Would you like a few minutes to go outside and prepare?" he asked.

"No. No, that's all right. I can do it right now," she responded.

And after saying this, Ms. Ivey closed her eyes. She very slowly turned away from us, put her hair up in a tight bun, and turned around to face the room. It took no longer than thirty seconds, but once again her body, her posture, the way she related to the air around her, had changed. The atmosphere of the room shifted with her. Once again, she nodded to Paul Ford at the piano, and she fearlessly launched into the Phyllis Stone material.

It was astonishing. Not a false note was sung or uttered. Ivey had such a deep understanding of the cold facade Phyllis wears in order to cover up her broken heart and broken dreams. Phyllis is the polar opposite of Sally: cool, controlled, calculating, and hard.

Ms. Ivey thanked us for the opportunity. We thanked her for her work. The room remained still and silent for a while after she left.

Without a doubt, Mr. Warchus knew he must cast her in the show. She landed the role of Sally Durant Plummer.

It was clear that Ms. Ivey did a very thorough study of the text in preparation for this audition. She understood who these characters were at their very core; how they thought; why they spoke the way they did, using language in their own individual and specific way. She understood how they moved, where they held their weight, how they related to the space around them. Most importantly, she understood the characters' objectives (what they wanted) and how to use the other person in the scene to get what she wanted. Finally, Ivey was excited to show us how she could portray these women. She wasn't concerned about getting it "right." She managed to accomplish this while bringing herself to the character instead of the other way around.

More recently, I was casting the Broadway revival of *Romeo and Juliet* starring Orlando Bloom and Condola Rashād. The process of making this production happen is a book in and of itself. It was in development for over three years.

I flew to Los Angeles to work with Mr. Bloom in June 2012. We spent a week going through the text, talking about objectives, tactics, and actions. We discussed the relationships between Romeo and the other characters in the play in connection to his main objective, which we defined, simply, as "to fly towards the sun."

Wait. Why isn't his objective about Juliet, you ask? His super-objective cannot be about Juliet, because, upon Romeo's first entrance in the play, he hasn't even *seen* her yet. He can't come on stage playing to win someone he doesn't even know. But if you perform a careful analysis of the text, you will find a plethora of both sun and flying imagery. Once he finds Juliet, she becomes his sun. This is why it's helpful as an actor to jot down the recurring themes or images you come across when reading a play you're working on, even if you're only focusing on a monologue from a larger text. This is also why it's important to pay attention to the *words* the playwright uses.

Bloom is a physical actor, and we spent a lot of time playing on our feet, finding the scenes through physical action as well as language. Getting Romeo into his body helped get Bloom out of his head. Also, the very simple and stimulating objective—to fly toward the sun— gave him a place to start from that sparked his imagination, was very actable, and influenced his physical life. His heart was always open and reaching up.

I worked with Bloom again in NYC for a few days, and then he flew to London to audition for David Leveaux, our director. He landed the role. That was in July 2012.

We did an initial round of casting in July and August of that year, seeing actors for a variety of the supporting roles. As we were securing official dates (as well as a Juliet!), we could only audition actors and tell them we were interested in them. We couldn't make offers. We couldn't tell them actual production dates. We couldn't tell them anything for certain, not even who our Romeo was. Many of these actors were not officially called back until January 2013, which is when Ms. Rashād (whose first audition was in August) landed the Juliet role after four auditions in New York and one in Los Angeles with Bloom.

Some actors never even had a callback. I was in constant contact with agents and managers from July 2012 to May 2013, letting them know we were still interested in their clients; that there might or might not be another round of callbacks; that they should let me know immediately if their client had another job offer, et cetera. And all the while, I was auditioning new people for parts we hadn't seen earlier. The show required a cast of twenty-three on-stage actors and one off-stage standby for Bloom.

Putting the Capulet and Montague families together was like a puzzle: headshots spread out on a long folding table as we weighed the pros of each actor, their look, and their qualities. All of these factors influence the production as a whole. Official offers were not made until May 2013.

I tell you this to illustrate how you, the actor, never know what goes on behind the scenes. Ultimately, you have no power over it. The only power you have is how you present yourself to the room as a person and a performer.

With rehearsal quickly approaching in July 2013, we had one role left to cast: Sampson, a servant of the House of Capulet. The actor playing this part would also understudy Justin Guarini, who played Paris. By the time we were in final callbacks for this small role, I had prescreened (an audition with just the actor and casting director, preceding a director's callback) or checked the availability of some four hundred actors for the part. Four hundred actors for a role that had approximately three lines of dialogue.

David Leveaux is attracted to actors who have strong personalities and who bring that into the room. The male casting for this production depended on virile, strong, playful men who also happened to be skilled in speaking verse, as David puts it, "on the line." That means speaking the lines as written and not adding unnecessary pauses or breaks in between every thought or word, allowing the action of the line to take you to the poetry instead of vice versa.

Our Sampson, a young man by the name of Donte Bonner, was all of these things and more. He walked into the room calm, collected, and in control. He enjoyed the process of auditioning. Bonner was excited to show us what he could do with the role, not preoccupied with hoping we liked him. This attitude is immediately attractive in an actor. On top of this, Bonner brought his own unique point of view to the character he was reading for. He was simple, specific, and alive. He was also skilled at taking direction. Although he had a very strong idea of his own, he was able to adjust when David asked for something completely different.

You can achieve the same level of performance as Ms. Ivey or Mr. Bonner if you put the requisite amount of work into your monologue, ask yourself the right questions (and the questions I ask you to examine following each of the pieces in this book), and activate your imagination.

Introduction
Approaching the Monologue

Actors are interpretive storytellers. We often forget that.

You take the words the writer has given you and process them through your own unique instrument (your mind, your body, your imagination, and, hopefully, your heart and your soul), and you turn those words into action—into doing. I'm sure you've been taught by this point in your career that acting is doing. As a teacher, acting coach, and director, I am constantly asking the questions "What are you doing?" and "Why are you doing that?" This doesn't mean a *physical* action. It means how are you *actively pursuing* your objective?

I'm also always asking the question "What does that mean?"

Most beginning actors think that memorizing the lines is enough. Or that emoting is enough. As I tell my undergraduate students, acting is hard work, and it's more than just memorizing lines and saying them out loud. It takes emotional connection, analytical skill, and an understanding of human behavior and relationships—as well as a relationship with language—to turn the written word into honest, believable action. Remember, any playwright worth his/her salt takes great care in choosing the language a character uses. In a well-written play, each character speaks differently. It is your job to find the key to unlocking the meaning of that language while giving it your own personal spin.

Rehearsing a monologue is tricky business, because you don't physically have a partner in front of you to work off of, react to, and actually affect. Oftentimes you'll find yourself staring at an empty chair, saying the lines out loud over and over. Hopefully, what follows will help you deepen your rehearsal process and activate your imagination. Imagination is one of the strongest abilities an actor can possess. If you can enter a room and create a specific, believable world in two minutes, we will trust that you can sustain that world for two-plus hours on a stage or in front of a camera.

You're reading this book because you're looking for an audition piece. It might be for a non-Equity or community-theater production, an undergraduate or graduate program, or a professional meeting with an agent or casting director. It may even be for an EPA.[1] Whatever the case, you're looking for a piece that—I hope—you feel you connect with on some level; that expresses a particular essence of you; that shows off your sense of humor or sense of self; and that, above all, tells a story you want to tell.

Your monologue choice tells the person (or sometimes the numerous people) behind the table something about you. Certainly it lets us know that you can stand in front of an audience, comfortable in your own body, and perform. It tells us you can open your mouth and speak someone else's words with meaning, confidence, and a sense of ease. It lets us know whether or not you have the ability to project or modify your voice depending on the requirements of the space.

More than that, your monologue choice tells us something about who you are as a person. Your monologue can tell us the type of things you respond to emotionally, intellectually, and humorously. After all, we're going under the assumption that you put a lot of time and care into finding a piece that you wanted to perform. You took the time to commit that piece to memory and to heart. You've imbued it with your

---

1   EPA stands for Equity Principal Auditions. All productions that produce on a contract with Actors Equity Association are required to have these calls. The casting department for these EPAs can provide scenes from the play they are casting or request monologues.

sense of humor, understanding, compassion, pain, and so on. More than just telling us whether or not you can act—and a monologue is by no means the only arbiter of this—the monologue helps us decide if we like you as a person, if you're someone we want to work with, study with, teach, and hire.

The monologue is, then, a reflection of you. What do you want us to know about you? This is why not every monologue works for every actor. Choose carefully. If it doesn't feel right, it most likely isn't. If you think it's a possibility, commit to the piece, do all of the work you can on it, and then perform it for people whose opinions you trust—not just people who tell you everything you do is wonderful (as nice as it is to have those people around). Ask someone who can be honest and helpfully critical.

Our first impulse is to ask, "Did you like it? How was I?"

Unfortunately, "like" is subjective. I can *not* like something yet still be affected by it. Instead, ask questions such as the following: "What did you learn about me from that? What do you think it says about who I am? What was the story? Could you tell what my objective was? Who was I? Did I take you on a journey? Was it playing on different levels, or did it seem too one-note?"

Then take it to a more businesslike level from there: "What am I selling? Does it play to my strengths? What weaknesses are on display in this piece? Does it seem 'type'-appropriate? Did I display a sense of strength as well as vulnerability?"

I will discuss some of these issues further in the pages that follow. However, it's important for an actor of any age to realize that you are selling yourself, and so you need to think like a businessperson. Play to your strengths and overcome your weaknesses. And if you can't overcome your weaknesses, learn how to cover them up! For example, if you can't cry on cue, don't pick a piece that requires you to do so. If you're terrible at telling jokes, don't end your monologue on a punch line.

So, you're a storyteller, an interpreter, and a businessperson. I told you acting was hard work. Pursue this career with an open heart and a tough skin, because for all the applause you'll receive, you'll also receive a lot of criticism and rejection. You have no control over *why* you did or didn't get cast. You do have control over your performance in the room. Focus on telling the story, a story you connect deeply to, and that's a safe and sure foundation.

Now let's begin.

Why Monologues?

Monologues give us a sense of your skill level and your personality.

As a professional casting director, I can think of only two instances in which I've asked actors to prepare a monologue for an audition. The first was when casting the Broadway production of Andrew Lloyd Webber's musical *The Woman in White*, directed by Trevor Nunn. All the actors coming into the room, whether auditioning for a leading role or a place in the ensemble, were asked to prepare music from the show, a contrasting song of their choice, and a Shakespearean monologue. Mr. Nunn, a Shakespearean expert, used the monologue as a way to get to know the actors, direct them, and gauge their ability to handle language and to play objectives and actions. I received a number of calls from agents, managers, and actors saying that they were uncomfortable with Shakespeare and maybe they shouldn't come in. However, I assured them this was the way Mr. Nunn worked, and he wouldn't be judging the actors' ability to handle the language requirements of Shakespeare but rather their ability to tell a story and take direction.

The second instance was when casting the Broadway revival of *Cyrano de Bergerac*. David Leveaux, the director, asked the men coming in for smaller roles, such as the poets and the soldiers, to prepare a classical monologue. In this instance, casting *was* dependent on the actors' ability to handle classical language. We were also able to assign understudy roles from these auditions because, based on the actors' monologue choice, we had a sense of who they were and of their technical and emotional abilities.

Now, that's two instances of using monologues in a more than fifteen-year career in casting. Truth to tell, I don't like monologue auditions. Although they give me a sense of who you are, they don't tell me if you can really act. I know some great actors who are terrible with monologues, and vice versa. Real acting is about collaboration. The true test of an actor is how they perform when faced with a director, another cast member, scenic and lighting elements, props, et cetera. You can be a brilliant performer when on your own and completely crash and burn when faced with a partner to whom you need to be open and receptive.

Nonetheless, as a college professor, I've learned that monologues are very important. Actors use them to audition for a program; we use them for season auditions within the department; and most importantly, my graduating seniors are asked to perform their monologues when they meet with agents and managers after their showcase.

Why? For all the reasons I've previously stated: Do you have the ability to speak with confidence and clarity? Do you have the ability to create a two-minute storytelling and emotional arc? Are you comfortable in your body? Can you play an objective? Can you play an action? Are you in control of your emotional life? Are you someone I want to spend time and work with? A monologue lets us know *who you are*. So it's important that you *know* who you are. And you don't have to be *one* thing, but again, know your strengths.

There appears to be an unwritten rule in schools that urges people away from "storytelling" monologues. In my experience, though, people are at their most active, engaged, and emotionally connected when they are sharing a personal experience. In this book you will find storytelling monologues for this very reason. What you must keep in mind in the performing of them is that we tell stories for a reason. Through these stories, the characters are trying to tell us something about themselves. Therefore, you're telling us something about *you* when you perform it. It's up to you to decide what that is, but make certain you feel emotionally connected to the piece and that you keep it active and engaged with a clear objective.

Now, in the monologues that don't necessarily contain an obvious "story," what do I mean by "storytelling"? I mean you are giving us a brief glimpse into the larger story of that character. You are living out the experience of—bringing to life—a very specific instance in the life of that character. Your plotting of that experience still needs to have a beginning, middle, and end. You must chart your emotional arc for these pieces just as you would if it were a traditional story. Take us on a journey, just the same.

CAUTION: Try not to beat us over the head by living in one extreme emotion for two minutes and simply playing one tactic the entire time. If you do this, your monologue will become monotonous and we will stop listening. Inexperienced actors sometimes think that simply crying or yelling or any generalized emoting is acting. If the character is still talking, it means they haven't achieved their objective yet. And if they haven't achieved their objective yet, it means that they haven't exhausted their arsenal of tactics yet. And if they haven't, you haven't.

Choosing a Monologue

I hope you've come to this book as a starting point. The best way to choose a monologue is to read plays. Read lots and lots of plays. Read every play you can get your hands on. Watch movies and television shows. Searching for—and preparing—monologues requires lots of work. Also, it's your job.

Why should you do all this work? The reasons are plenty, but let me expound upon a few of them.

1. Playwrights are the reason we, as theater professionals, exist. It is our job to honor their work while bringing it to life. You will soon find yourself gravitating to a certain writer or writers. You will want to perform their work. You will seek out productions of theirs wherever you are in the country or the world. You will, eventually, want to work with this playwright and help create new work or revive previous work. You will want to interpret and tell their stories. And—if you move to a city like New York, Los Angeles, or Chicago—you will most likely come into contact with them at some point in time and you can speak with them about their work with knowledge and breadth.

   Conversely, there will be writers you find you don't connect with at all. If this is the case, do not use monologues from their work. You need to love the piece on some very basic level. So even if you can't define why you're not a fan, move on. Pick up the play a few months or years later and read it again. Maybe you'll come at it from a different perspective and it will connect with you. It may never.

   Finally, many of these playwrights you love and admire get hired to write, produce, and run television shows. Whether in New York or L.A., you will come across a writer who has moved from theater to the film industry for any number of reasons (money). You will find, I bet, their heart still remains in the theater, and they will love to hear you are a fan of theirs.

2. You'll come across monologues that aren't right for you at this point in your life but can be put on the shelf and pulled out again when you're in your late twenties, early thirties, forties, or even sixties. Yes, people in their fifties and sixties still audition, no matter who or where they are. The work, if you're lucky, never ends.

3. When you read these plays and watch TV shows and films, you're researching. You're finding out which actors are getting cast in

the parts you want to play. Follow their careers. This is how you begin to track and define your "type." This is how you learn what parts are out there for you. The cast list that precedes the play in most published work is a guide for you. Google the actors and find out who they are and what they've done.

The actress Saidah Arrika Ekulona (you don't know who she is? Google her. It's your job) spoke to my students recently and said, "Don't worry about so much about your type. Don't obsess about it. Somebody, somewhere is ready to put you in a box, so why should you do it for yourself?" I wholeheartedly agree—and disagree—with her! Here's where I agree: of course you must believe you can do anything, play any part. You need to constantly raise the bar for yourself so that you have goals to work toward. Just because you're the "ingénue" or "the leading man" doesn't mean you can't also find the humor, sexuality, and hunger in those roles. You need to find the complexities and polarities in every role you play. People are complicated, and therefore so are characters.

However, you also need to keep in mind that this is a business. And people in business want to know how you're marketable. So if you have a list of actors who are doing the things you know how to do, playing the parts you know you can play, you are armed with information that's going to help you market yourself. Don't think of defining your type as a "box." It's not. It's a marketing strategy.

It may sound like a cliché, but knowledge is power. And your knowledge of these plays, writers, and fellow actors is your weapon. Put it to use.

4. Films and TV are fair game when searching for material. However, you want to stay away from material that would be considered "iconic." Avoid characters that are firmly ingrained in our popular

culture. Shows like *Girls*, *Sex and the City*, or *Friends* have great writing, but that writing became more and more tailored to the specific actors playing those roles as the seasons progressed. It is difficult to approach that material without hearing the voices of those original actors in our heads. So enjoy those shows, but don't use them, even if your type is a Carrie, a Charlotte, a Joey, or a Chandler.

5. Sometimes you'll find a character that you really like but who doesn't have a stand-alone monologue in the play. You'll be tempted to cut and paste the lines together until you form it into something that seems complete. I caution you away from this. Although some of the pieces in this book have been edited, there has been no major cutting and rearranging. I find that it destroys the author's intent. You're crafting a piece into something it wasn't meant to be. Look at something else by this writer. Or search for a similar character in another play. Your "type" work will come in handy here. The actor who played this role was also in what other plays? This writer has also written what other plays?

6. Once you've chosen a monologue from this book (or from a play or film), please read the entire work. Then read it again. Then— read it again. Although you will ultimately be performing the piece out of context, you can act it well only if you can make sense of the context in which it was written.

Preparing the Monologue

I am asking you to do a lot of work here. But if this monologue leads to landing a job or an agent or gets you into the grad school of your choice, then you want to do as much preparation as possible to make it a complete, worthwhile experience for you and the people behind the table.

I've heard from many actors over the years that they don't want to be "over-rehearsed." They want to keep their piece "fresh." If you feel your piece is over-rehearsed, then you are doing something wrong. There is no such thing. The amount of work that goes into keeping a piece fresh and alive is endless. Ask someone who has been in a Broadway show for six months, or a year. There is always something more to unearth in a role, especially if you keep clarifying and refining your objective, actions, and relationships.

Here's how to start.

1. Read the entire play.
2. Read the entire play again.
3. Read it one more time.
4. Although you will have been very tempted to do so, do *not* read the monologue out loud yet. You've read the play a few times now, and you're beginning to, consciously or unconsciously, realize the intention of the piece in the whole.
5. Have a notebook handy to write down your initial thoughts, reactions, and responses to the play, the characters, and the relationships.

I want you to think about the play as a whole, first, by asking these questions:

Is this a dramatic or a comedic monologue?

This is a tough question. I find that most good monologues walk the line between the two, putting them in the "seriocomic" category. A comedic monologue is not always about landing a joke. A comedic monologue shows that you can handle material that is light and playful while still playing a strong objective and having an emotional connection to the text. A dramatic monologue tackles more serious issues, events, and emotions. Be careful that your dramatic monologue doesn't dissolve into you screaming and/or crying in the direction of the auditioner. This is *not* a sign that you can act. If you're crying and screaming, then you are most likely not playing toward an objective while using strong actions. You're just being self-indulgent.

In life, we rarely get what we want when we scream or cry at people. It's no different in acting.

What are some of the major themes of the play?

It is often easiest to define your character's objective by wording it to include the main themes or images in the play.

Themes are the major ideas or topics of the play, together with the writer's point of view on these topics. Sometimes the theme will reveal itself through repetition of imagery, such as the sun and flight imagery I mentioned earlier in *Romeo and Juliet*.

Make a list of these themes, both major and minor, in your notebook.

What does the title of the play mean?

The author's intention or point of view is often most clearly defined in the title of the play. Thinking about it might also lead you to define the main theme of the work, as just discussed. Your work on the theme of the play should lead you directly here.

Who is the main character in the play?

Whose story is it? What is their journey? If you're performing a monologue of the main character, how does the piece affect their progression? If you're performing a piece from a supporting character, how does it assist or impede the main character's journey?

The main character is the person who takes the biggest journey over the course of the play. Your monologue is one of the following: (1) the person on that journey; (2) a person helping the main character on that journey; (3) a person creating an obstacle to the main character achieving their goal.

Even in an ensemble play, there is always a main character.

What is your objective?

This question is twofold, because I'm asking you to define your objective for both the play and the monologue. You need to define what this character wants throughout the entire play—from the moment he or she steps onto the stage. Then you need to define how this two-minute (or so) piece fits into the whole.

An objective is a *simple, active, positive* statement that defines the journey your character is on.

It is in defining an objective that most young actors tend to hinder their performance. You never want to define your objective in the following ways: (1) I want "to *be* something," or (2) I want "to *feel* something." These are passive, inactive statements in which you will not make any forward progression. Emotion does play a role in acting, but not when it comes to defining an objective.

Instead I want you to define it in very vivid, active words that inspire you and spark your imagination. This is where your knowledge of the entire play and the character you are creating comes into action.

Begin by thinking in very primal terms. Objectives should hold life-or-death stakes: companionship, shelter, protection, nourishment, sex, fight, and flight.

"I want to hold my family together" is a very strong objective.

"I want to make someone love me" is another.

However, I challenge you to take it a step further. If you're working on Mona Pirnot's *Lessons from an Abandoned Work*, you might start with "I want to learn as much as possible." But you can use the language and the imagery from the play, taking your objective into deeper territory: "I want to uncover as many mysteries about the hidden human condition as possible." The more vividly you can paint the objective, especially by using words and images from the play itself, the better.

Play your objective with the belief that you're going to WIN! Play positive choices. We don't go to the theater to see people lose. We want to see them try to overcome. Even if they don't succeed.

I can't stress enough that every time you step in front of someone to act, you must have an objective. Every time. Whether you're performing a monologue, a song, or an entire play, you must have an objective. It's one of the basic conditions of acting. If you don't have an objective, you don't have a goal, and there's no reason to act (or to watch). Even if you find out that objective doesn't work, commit to it while you're performing and then try something else the next time.

I have asked many an actor in an audition what their objective was only to get silence in return. Not every casting director is going to do this and then give you another chance. Figure out what you want to *do* before you come into the room. Otherwise, you're wasting your time and ours.

What are the beats and actions?

A *beat* is a transition: a change in thought, action, subject, or tactic.

Not every line is a new beat. Try to find it organically. When it feels like there is a shift in thought, there most likely is. That is your beat. Trust your instincts. Are you accomplishing what you want? Are you winning? If not, it's time to shift your tactic.

Have you been playing the same tactic over and over without achieving your goal? It's time to shift your tactic. Backtrack: when did that start? How can you adjust?

Actions are active verbs that define what you are doing in any particular moment. Meaning, you attach an active verb to every line of text: to sway, to punish, to defend, to challenge, and so on.

Actions become your roadmap, your markers. If you're a musician, think of them as musical notes. The note is written there, but it's up to you to color it, make it your own, and endow it with meaning. Engage your own unique point of view to make it personal. However, every new action does not necessarily mean you've come to a beat change. Again, feel it out instinctively. You should have an action for every line. Hard work, I know. However, this work makes you really pay attention to the language of the play and the words you are using to achieve your objective.

You cannot consciously play these objectives, beats, actions, and tactics, but you must rehearse with them in mind so that you can internalize them. Once they've become internalized, they will play themselves. It's a form of muscle memory. The challenge then becomes to trust that the work is there and let it go.

Check in with your (imaginary) scene partner. Make sure your actions are landing. This is where your imagination comes into play. When you look at the empty space you have to see how they're reacting, how they're looking (or not looking) at you.

Playing actions helps in two areas: it helps you do more than play the "mood" of the piece. Mood is established in the arc of the storytelling, not in the way you say the lines. Mood is also established in how you're relating to the other person: are you winning, or losing? Secondly, playing actions will help you not play the end of the monologue at the beginning. If the monologue ends in death, you don't want us to know that when you start. Take us there without letting us know we're going to get there.

When I was working as the assistant director of Martin McDonagh's Broadway production of A *Behanding in Spokane*, John Crowley, the director, would sit at the table with the actors every afternoon after lunch and make them assign actions to every line of text. We did this for weeks. It is oftentimes very frustrating, but it lets you know where you're going. It forces you into specificity. And if any particular action doesn't seem to work for you, throw it out and try another! That is why actors rehearse.

Right now you're asking yourself why you need to do all of this work. Let's go back to the words that opened this book: Actors are storytellers, and the best stories are those told with specificity. Think of this monologue as a smaller story inside a larger one. You need to understand the larger story the playwright is telling in order to tell this shorter story. You need to know the details in order to bring them to life.

The greater your understanding of the piece as a whole, the better your ability to interpret it. Doing all of this work doesn't take all the fun out of performing. The more information we have, the deeper we can go and the more fun we can have. Specificity leads to freedom.

Remember, people rarely expect to speak in monologue form. Have an expectation of how you think your (unseen) partner may react. This is part of a conversation, and your partner is letting you speak for quite a bit of time, or you are not letting them get a word in. Don't approach it as a monologue; approach it as dialogue. Expect your scene partner to cut you off. Your expectation is key to why you go on for some two minutes. Pay attention to and play with your partner. Oftentimes this expectation of interruption will help you bring a sense of urgency to the piece.

Inevitably, you will be performing these monologues for someone who knows the play. You want your acting of the monologue to be consistent with the tone, theme, and style of the play, as well as with the character's objective within it. You can't take a monologue from *Macbeth*, for example, and mine it for high comic potential. You'll look foolish, and the casting director will assume you don't know what you're doing.

Who is your character?

Once you've answered all of the above questions, it's time to start putting this person into your body.

1. What do they look like?
2. How do they dress?
3. How do they stand?
4. Where is their center of gravity?
5. How do they take up space?
6. What's their posture?
7. Where does their voice sit (i.e., head, throat, chest, diaphragm, etc.)?
8. Where do they hold tension?
9. How do they walk, sit, and stand?

It's up to you to find this person in your body—experiment with them. Holding on to what you know about them from the script, and your very strong objective, you'll be able to find physicality for them through your knowledge of them.

If you can imagine them, you can become them.

Whom is your character talking to?

These are monologues, but you need to have a very specific picture of *whom* you are talking to, because it plays directly into *why* you are talking (your objective). Some of these monologues are to a specific person, or persons; some were written as audience address. You still need to decide to whom, specifically, it is directed and have a clear image of that person.

Place that person somewhere in the room with you. You should never perform your monologue directly to the person for whom you are auditioning unless they ask. You can place them, in your imagination, to the left or the right and a little in front of that person. You can place them behind that person and a little above their head. You can place them closer to you, to your immediate left, right, or center. However, make sure that they're not so close that you are forced to look down while you deliver your monologue. We need to see your face.

Now that you've placed your "acting partner" somewhere, you need to imagine what they look like.

1. What are they wearing?
2. Are they sitting, or standing?
3. What is your relationship to them?
4. What do you need from them? (This ties in to your objective)
5. How is delivering this monologue bringing you closer to achieving your goal?
6. By the end of the monologue, did you win? Did you get what you wanted? Are you closer or further away from achieving you goal?

If you can imagine the acting partner vividly and specifically, we will see them.

What's so urgent?
Younger actors often lack a sense of urgency. Remember, your character is dealing with life-and-death stakes! Urgent doesn't mean "do it quickly." Urgent means: why do you need to say these things right now? Why do you need to achieve your objective right now? What just happened that makes every word in this monologue so important? This should carry life-or-death stakes: *If I don't achieve this objective right now, my life will fall apart.*

Using the language to your advantage (covered in a section that follows) will guarantee that you can add heat to your monologue without rushing through.

The quality of your time on stage is much more important than the quantity. Please don't think that the longer you take, the more illustrative you're being.

Emotional Connection

Up until now I have hardly mentioned feelings, emotions, or emoting. You must, of course, have a strong emotional connection to the monologue you choose. Your connection may grow or dissipate when you complete the work outlined above. Sometimes the more you discover about a play, or a character, the further it feels from your initial response. If this is the case, and you can't reclaim that initial spark, then move on to something else. You can always find another piece.

Conversely, your initial response to the monologue might be only so-so until you do more work on it, finding yourself truly enlivened and engaged by it. In that case, take it and run.

Acting is not about emoting. Young actors tend to find pieces with very high emotional stakes that often require crying or screaming in order to accomplish the storytelling. Please shy away from these. We want to see that you are emotionally connected to the material and that you know how to *control* your emotional life. We do not want to have your emotions unleashed upon us in a flood that you cannot contain. Therefore, a monologue that occurs at the climax of a play is probably best left performed in the context of the show.

After performing all of the work laid about above, your emotional connection to the piece should be growing organically. You relation-ship to the character, his/her objective, the relationships, and the story should be incredibly strong. You should find yourself invested in living through the experience and sharing the story.

If you feel that you are still generating (read: *forcing*) an emotional reaction in order to make the monologue work for you, I would suggest putting it aside. You don't want us to see you working hard in order to put the material over.

Language and Point of View

I've talked a lot about your relationship to language and how you need to have one. Words and punctuation, as provided by the writer, can sometimes unlock the key to your character. Language is how these characters express what they need. Please use the words to your advantage.

Nothing about the language is secondary. If there weren't words, there wouldn't be a story.

Remember that acting occurs *on* the lines, not in between them. Try to express what you're feeling by coloring a word or a phrase with your point of view while maintaining the flow of the line. Tie your thoughts together without breaking the line apart in pieces in an attempt to highlight certain words.

The line is your thought and your action: present it completely. Try not to add moments, beats, unexpressed thoughts, and feelings in between the lines. It's not necessary. Use what the playwright has given you.

If the playwright wants you to take time somewhere, they will provide the clues. It can be as specific as them writing *pause* or *beat*.

There are other clues, though:

An ellipsis (. . .) often signifies a trailing off of thought or a search for the right thing to say.

A hyphen or dash (—) often signifies a break in thought, a cut-off thought, or a new idea.

These are basically the only times you have permission to break up the thought. Otherwise, see your energy through the entire line. Stay engaged and alive, and keep the thought moving.

A word or a line written in all caps means the author wants you to highlight that particular section, but it does not necessarily mean you need to yell and scream it.

Be aware of repetition. If a writer uses the same word or phrase repeatedly, they're trying to tell you something. How you shade that word (or don't) each time it comes up says something about the character and what they're after.

Also, pay attention to periods, question marks, exclamation points, and other basic punctuation marks. These are not arbitrary. Something delivered as a statement has a completely different meaning if it's intended to be delivered as a question. This isn't your decision to make if the writer has shown otherwise.

Some playwrights (Adam Bock, for example) take away almost all punctuation. He is specifically writing characters searching for their point of view, unable to make decisions, living in a world of ambivalence. You need to commit to each of these thoughts, but he's leaving it up to you to figure out what each could be.

Point of view is how you (your character) see the world, relate to the people and objects around you, and relate to language. This is where artistry occurs. Anyone can say the words. How you give them meaning, how you filter all of this through your perspective, is what makes your interpretation unique.

Also what is your point of view on the person to whom you're speaking? This has to go deeper than "I like him" or "I don't like her." Who is she to you? "My sister," for example, is a surface definition. "This is the one person in the world I've shared all my secrets with my entire life" takes it a step further. "This is the one person in the world I've shared all my secrets with in my entire life, but she's never had her heart broken and doesn't understand how I'm feeling" takes it even further. More importantly, can this person help you achieve your objective, or are they standing in your way?

Your point of view must be apparent when you talk about a person or a place that has an emotional effect on you: your mother, your father, your sister, or your brother. Or you could be speaking about your childhood home or your favorite restaurant. How do you feel about them? Where in your body do you feel them when you speak about them?

Point of view is what makes the character *yours*.

Edit

You can't have everything. You can't make every moment last a lifetime. All of the tools I've provided you with are an effort to keep you active and engaged and in the moment. If you find yourself lingering over a word, a phrase, a pause, I want you to ask yourself *why*. Is it necessary? Are you staying true to the storytelling, the author's intention, and the character's objective? Will hanging out in that moment help you achieve your objective faster, better, with more urgency? Will screaming, crying, and wailing do the same? In both cases, probably not.

Finally, it's time for you to put all of the pieces together. You have all the elements of the story, and now you need to get from point A, to point B, to point C. This takes a long rehearsal process. It means experimenting with all of these elements. If something does not work, throw it away and try something else. If something seems to maybe, kind of work, hold on to it and experiment inside of that. Try doing the entire piece in a whisper and see what you learn. Try doing it at the top of your voice in a public place and see what you discover. Take risks with how you rehearse it and you might find something you never knew was there.

I strongly urge you *not* to practice these monologues in front of a mirror. It will only make you feel self-conscious, and you will put your focus and energy into how you look while you do it rather than into what you are *doing*. Instead, practice it in front of friends and family. Practice achieving your objective on them. Practice your actions on them.

You have created a roadmap, but that doesn't mean you can't take side trips. Your objective is in mind; now try a roundabout way of getting there. Remember, these are called "plays," and you should, in fact, play. Have fun.

In Performance

You are ready to perform the monologue in public. Here are a few quick tips for the audition room:

Some actors think it doesn't matter how they present themselves when they enter or exit the audition room. Your audition starts the moment the door opens and doesn't end until you leave.

1. Arrive early. At least fifteen minutes before your appointment time. You need this time to unclutter your mind, focus yourself, and relax.

2. When your name is called, close your eyes and take a deep breath in and out. Find your center.

3. Take as few of your personal items into the room as necessary. Try not to bring in your jacket, your bag, your purse, your gym clothes, and so on. Gentlemen, please take phones, keys, and loose change out of your front pockets; do not interrupt the natural line of your body.

4. Say a friendly "Hello" to the person or persons in the room, even if they seem engaged in another activity. Very often, we are writing notes about whoever just exited, but we will try to make contact and greet you, the next person entering the room, especially to see if you look like your headshot.

5. Look like your headshot.

6. Leave your bitterness, your disappointment, and your desperation outside of the door. There's no room for it in the audition. We can sense all of them. If you put your energy into your emotions

instead of into telling the story, you will not get cast. This is a business, like any other, filled with unfairness and disappointments. Don't take it out on the people behind the table. Don't sabotage yourself. The only thing that matters is the work. You can bitch to your friends later. But we can sense your negativity, and we don't want it.

7. Do not advance on the table, introduce yourself, and attempt to shake hands. Keep a friendly, professional distance unless the person behind the table makes a move otherwise. We sometimes see a hundred people in one day; we can't shake everyone's hand.

8. Be nice to everyone in the room, including the reader and the accompanist. We take note of that. Remember we're looking to form an ensemble, and how you treat every everyone matters. Also remember that today's accompanist is tomorrow's up-and-coming composer.

9. Do not apologize for what you're about to do or explain that you:
   a. Are sick.
   b. Have just been sick.
   c. Feel as if you're getting sick.

10. Find a comfortable space to stand, or ask for a chair if you're using one. There will almost always be a chair available for you. It makes no difference to us whether you stand or sit, but it sometimes makes a difference to your monologue.

11. Once you're in position, please introduce yourself and let us know the title of the play from which the monologue comes.

12. Take a moment before you begin. Close your eyes or turn away from us. Center yourself. Runners don't hit the track and begin running. They take their position, they focus themselves, they wait for the gun, and then they go. In this situation, you are in charge of the gun. The room is yours when you walk in. As you arrived some fifteen minutes before entering the room, this

shouldn't take more than a second or two. Please, no slumping in place, no shaking out your arms and legs, no vocalizing. All of this should be done at home or outside the room. The moment before is simply to focus.

13. Act! Have fun. We want you to be good. We want to welcome you into our program, our school, and our cast. Worry less about getting it "right" and concentrate on telling us a story.

13a. Sometimes you start off on the wrong foot. That's okay. You can stop and ask if you can start again. Take a breath. Focus. Start again. If it doesn't happen the second time, you should kindly apologize and leave the room. You're not prepared. You've not done enough work on the piece, or you're letting your nerves get the better of you. There are no tried-and-true tricks for beating this. Comfort and familiarity with the material, combined with a desire to tell the story, are your best bets!

14. Keep it to two minutes. All of the monologues in this book fulfill that requirement, and some are shorter. You do not need to use the entire two minutes. We can very often tell if we're interested in someone within the first thirty seconds to a minute.

15. When you've finished, take a beat and end the piece. Give us a cue that your performance is over and you're no longer the character. Again, be careful of judging your work while in the room. I've seen many actors want to apologize or make a face that says, "Well, that didn't go the way I had planned it." Whether it was your best work or your worst work, don't let us know.

16. There's a fine line between lingering and rushing out of the room. Sometimes we may ask you a question or two in an effort to get to know you better. Stay focused and centered until we say, "Thank you."

17. Your résumé should be a reflection of your work. Please don't lie on it in any way, shape, or form! Don't say you've worked with

people or on productions that you never have! If you were in the ensemble, don't say you were the lead! We've all been in the ensemble. It's okay.

18. Enjoy the storytelling.

In this book I'm providing you with a summary of the play, a brief character description, and a list of questions you should ask yourself when approaching the material. However, I urge you to seek out the play and read it in its entirety so that you can have a greater understanding of the character, the situations, and the events.

Most importantly, when performing any of these pieces, play a strong, simple, vivid objective; maintain a deep emotional connection to the material; act on the line; have a sense of urgency; and know why, and to whom, you're speaking.

Some of the monologues included in this volume are very short. I find it's helpful to have these in your back pocket in case you are asked to do something else and want something quick that packs a punch. As I said earlier, you can provide a good sense of what you can do in a relatively short amount of time.

Conversely, some of these pieces are long. I am providing you with alternate cuts within the larger structure that, I believe, maintain the original intent of the author and still provide storytelling opportunities.

Etiquette for Scene Study, Rehearsal, and Beyond

My recent experiences as a college professor and associate director led me to discover that some of the things I assumed were obvious (in regard to behavior, attitude, and work ethic) for actors of all ages and levels were, in fact, not.

The second you walk in the door, you are there to serve the work, not your ego.

No matter who you are in the show, you are part of an ensemble, and every move you make affects that. The ensemble extends to everyone working on the production: stage management, director, crew, stage door man, et cetera. Each of these people deserves your attention and respect.

I compiled this list in response to that discovery and have a feeling it will keep evolving over my lifetime and, hopefully, beyond. It might not necessarily serve you in an audition setting, but keep it in mind once you book the work.

First-Day-of-Rehearsal Behavior
- Be present. Everyone is nervous and excited.
  - Do not isolate yourself.
  - Approach individuals and introduce yourself.
  - Tell them what your role is (even if you're an understudy).
  - Make conversation by asking questions about the person you're speaking with, not reciting your resume.
  - Seek out the director, producer, and casting director and thank them for the opportunity.

- During the read-through, don't highlight your lines. *Listen* to the play.
- During the read-through, don't look ahead to see when you're next on stage. *Listen* to the play.

First Read-through and Every Rehearsal

- Dress appropriately
  - ○ Dress in a silhouette similar to your character's. If your character wears long pants, do not rehearse in shorts. If your character wears a skirt, wear a skirt.
  - ○ Do not wear clothing with logos or slogans printed on it. You want your partner focusing on you, your face, your body, and your behavior, *not* reading your T-shirt or laughing at the funny print on it.
  - ○ Do not wear open-toed shoes or sandals ever, unless the role requires them. Do not rehearse a fight scene in these shoes *ever*.
  - ○ Do not change your hair length, color, or style at any time before rehearsal starts or during the process without consulting your director first.
- Practice personal hygiene
  - ○ Brush your teeth before every rehearsal and after every break, especially after eating or smoking.
  - ○ Shower every day and before every performance.
  - ○ Wear clean clothes to rehearsal every day. If you wear the same things, figure out a way to wash them as much as possible.
  - ○ Go to the gym. Eight shows a week require strength and stamina. Film shoots can be long and exhausting.
  - ○ If you go to the gym before rehearsal, shower.
  - ○ Get seven to eight hours of sleep a night.
  - ○ Drink and smoke in moderation.

- Bring a pencil and paper with you. Every day. Have backups.
- Phones are not a place to take notes at any time during the process.
- Character idea: Have one based on an intelligent reading and analysis of the script.
- Your character idea should be flexible. The director may steer you in a different direction. Try it for a few days. If it doesn't feel right, explain this and use your reading and analysis of the script to support your case. Ultimately, your director has the final say.
- Don't emphasize pronouns and verbs. These are very often the least interesting words in the sentence.
- Don't be late. Give yourself time to arrive at least ten minutes early. You should be ready to work at start time, not arriving. If you need time to warm up, factor this into your travel time.
- *Listen.* Listen to everyone.
- Pay attention to what the director says about the world of the play. Even if it does not immediately give you information about your character specifically, he or she is sharing their vision of the show with you. You can very often pick up something valuable to use immediately or in the future as you create your character. This information informs your choices.
- Don't ask too many questions right away. Don't make everything about your character and you. The rehearsal process is one of discovery, and you shouldn't discover everything in the first week. Also, if you *listen*, you may discover the answers to your questions without having to ask.
- Look up the definition and pronunciation of any unfamiliar word or reference.
- Find an activity for every scene you're in. We rarely sit and talk. Activity creates behavior. This activity should be rooted in the text and what the text says you could or should be doing.

- Don't confuse your *fear* with your *process*. It is your job to take risks in rehearsal, and this doesn't always happen in your comfort zone or when you are ready to. *Jump* when the director asks you to without asking "How high?" first.
- Don't use the word "process" to defend your insecurities. The director has a process, too, and that's to get a performance out of you, and it doesn't always happen on your terms. Your "process" is not an excuse to not try something the director is asking.
- Unless otherwise instructed, be off-book the second time you get to a scene.
- Use the rehearsal room as your opportunity to *take chances*.
- Don't stand in your own way. Listen to the script and your director, not your ego.
- Don't enter a scene to "have a scene" with your partner. It's your job to keep that person in the room, and vice versa. You're coming in to achieve something, and the other person is either going to help or hinder you. Live truthfully within that knowledge.
- Always find a sense of urgency in your character.
- Always find a sense of humor in your character.

Men's Monologues

A Hard Rain
Jon Bradfield and Martin Hooper

JIMMY

Is this your office?

Businessmen get to travel places, don't they? You get to travel?

You could go to London, they changed the law there. You could open a joint. A real nice —

Oh. My dad did that to my shoulder.

And this is from when he put my arm through the window.

This I got from a cigarette setting my shirt on fire but I did that myself when I fell asleep in a doorway.

I don't see them no more. Well, I saw my mom three weeks ago. Went home to see if there was food there, and my brother, cos I like my brother, but they don't like me being around my brother. I'm a 'bad kid.'

I'm not though.

You can go back down to the bar now if you want. I'll let myself out.

Analysis: *A Hard Rain*

Type: Dramatic
Synopsis
"This city's got everything that's right and everything that's wrong in it. And every day you gotta choose what kinda man you are."

It's June 1969 in Greenwich Village, New York—the era of Stonewall and Vietnam. Frank is attempting to open his fourth bar in two years. His last place was shut down after three weeks. The only way to keep a gay bar open in this time period is to pay off the cops, but the payments are getting so large that Frank can hardly afford them.

This new bar is called The Baker's Tavern, so named because it was formerly a bakery. The bar is run by Angie, a bartender and unwed mother. Frank has big plans for this place: a stage, a card table, roulette upstairs. Frank is married with a daughter about to enter college, but he has a penchant for underage street boys, like Jimmy.

Jimmy comes to the bar looking for something: whiskey, a place to hang, someone to sleep with, a trick, a friend. Frank recognizes him a former pickup who stole his wallet after Frank had paid him. Angie warns the young boy, who replies, simply: "I don't get hurt. It's just how things are."

Jimmy sleeps with Frank in order to land a job as his "assistant." Frank has him make deliveries of unspecified products for him, a really dangerous job. Jimmy does it hoping that one day he can be a bartender. Danny, a local cop, takes interest in Jimmy and tries to warn him about Frank. Jimmy doesn't listen but promises that he'll keep in contact with Danny, letting him know how it's going. Act 1 ends with the police raiding the bar.

Act 2 is about Frank trying to rebuild and reopen the bar. He finds out about Jimmy talking to Danny and, blaming Jimmy for the raid, has him killed and his body dumped in the river.

Character Description
Jimmy, 16 years old
Jimmy is a skinny sixteen-year-old who wears eyeliner and is desperate for a job and/or money. He dreams of one day marrying a soldier and likes to sing the song "Forget Me Not" by Martha and the Vandellas, because it's about a soldier coming home from war. When he was

thirteen, Jimmy had a boyfriend who was a cop. They lived together. Jimmy would cook breakfast every morning, and they would eat on the balcony. The cop would go to work, and Jimmy would go back to bed. It lasted one summer. His lesson on survival is simple: "Be pretty. Listen to his boring stories. Let him beat you about a bit. Steal his money." He does drugs and sometimes refers to himself as "Miss Jimmy."

Given Circumstances

Who are they? Frank is Jimmy's forty-something "boss."
Where are they? Frank's office above the bar.
When does this take place? 1969.
Why are they there? They've just had sex.
What is the pre-beat? Jimmy just did a line of cocaine.

Questions

1. Can you state your objective in a simple, specific, and active way?
2. Whom are you talking to? Be specific and have a clear image.
3. Can you think of three adjectives to describe your character?
4. How long have you been in NYC?
5. Where did you come here from?
6. How old were you when you got here?
7. When (and how) did you discover you could attract older men?
8. What does Frank look like?
9. Are you physically attracted to him?
10. How much money do you need to make to survive?
11. What was it like to be young and gay in 1969?
12. How often did your father beat you?
13. How many other bruises do you have?
14. Have you ever felt safe and protected?
15. Do you like having sex with older men?

Sondra
Laura Cahill

BUCKY

I couldn't come home and not turn on the TV. I gotta watch my
TV. I go right for it the minute I walk in the door. No matter
what I'm doing it's always on.

That's how I do things. People think "he works at Hess," and
they see all the glory. It's a good job, I know that, but I like to go
home and relax. When I was in high school I was the big wrestler.
I had the girl. I had the nicest car, went to a movie every Friday
night. Went to eat. I had my pants pressed and I did my hair, all
nice. Everyone saw me. What do I care? I can chill a little now.
I go to work, I watch TV.

I still do okay in the lady department. I got girls asking me out
all the time. I don't even have to do anything. Girls just call you
over to their car when they drive in to the station, they yell out
"Hi Bucky" that kind of thing. One chick takes pictures on her
phone while I'm filling her up, I'm like "what are you doing?"
Some of these girls do really crazy shit.

Analysis: *Sondra*

Type: Seriocomic
Synopsis
The action of the play takes place in working-class New Jersey. It's a town
dense in population, intersected by highways, and just out of reach of
anything special. It's the kind of place that would make anyone feel stuck.

Sondra is nineteen years old. She lives with Barb, her mother, in an old house at the end of a lonely street. Sondra works at the mall. She's the assistant manager of accessories at JCPenney, but she has plans to get out—out of this house and out of this town. Barb isn't going anywhere. She's a cocktail waitress, most likely born and raised in this town. She's divorced and on a manhunt. Barb has taken in a boarder for the spare bedroom, a working man named Joe. Joe works at Auto Parts Express on Route 9. He's also an assistant manager. Joe takes an instant liking to Sondra, not to Barb.

Barb is constantly trying to make money. Joe is a way to get more money in the house. She also has a side business in which she sells watches designed to "align your electric currents preventing negative takeover." In essence, scam watches that are supposed to prevent cancer. Joe asks Sondra out, leaves her notes, and becomes an uncomfortable and dangerous presence in the house for Sondra. Barb is unaware of this and won't listen to Sondra when Sondra asks for help.

Jennifer is Sondra's on-again/off-again best friend. Most of her peers find Sondra strange. She writes in her journal all the time. She's not man-crazy. She has dreams of getting out. Most people in this town dream of getting through the week so they can party all weekend. Jennifer is pregnant again and about to get an abortion. Sondra is stable, so Jennifer has gravitated towards her.

Joe keeps making advances on Sondra that she keeps dodging or rejecting. Joe begins to sell watches for Barb and invites Bucky over to make a sale. They end up just hanging out and drinking with the girls. Jennifer takes an immediate interest in Bucky, because he's a man. They play a game called "Truth or Lie," and Sondra gets very drunk. Jennifer goes for a ride with Bucky, leaving Joe and Sondra alone. Joe confronts Sondra about her being stuck up. In the final scene, Barb returns home from work to find Joe packing and leaving and Sondra gone. Jennifer returns without Bucky and sits on the stoop with Barb as they wait for Sondra. They're not aware of Joe's anger or intense feelings for Sondra.

Character Description
Bucky, late teens
Bucky is the assistant manager of the Hess Gas Station in town. Joe meets him there and tries to sell him an eco-watch, which is why Bucky comes over. Bucky isn't upset when the watch isn't there. He had nothing else to do and is happy to sit around and drink beer. He always has a TV on at home, no matter what he's doing. Joe asks him for advice on getting a lady, since Bucky is pretty popular. He drives a blue and white Dodge Ram.

Given Circumstances
Who are they? Joe and Bucky have just met.
Where are they? The kitchen of the house where Joe rents a room.
When does this take place? The present.
Why are they there? Joe is trying to sell Bucky an eco-watch.
What is the pre-beat? Bucky asked Joe if he watched anything good on TV, and Joe answered he doesn't own one at this time.

Questions
1. Can you state your objective in a simple, specific, and active way?
2. Whom are you talking to? Be specific and have a clear image.
3. Can you think of three adjectives to describe your character?
4. How long have you worked at the Hess station?
5. What are some of the everyday details of your job?
6. How long ago did you start there, and how long did it take to work your way up to assistant manager?
7. Do you like your job?
8. Describe the "glory" of your work.

9. Why can you "chill" more now than in high school?

10. What shows do you watch on TV?

11. Do you pick up a lot of women at your job?

12. Why did you come over to see Joe tonight?

13. Is this a nice house?

14. What conditions do you live in?

15. How many times in your life have you left New Jersey?

The Day I Stood Still
Kevin Elyot

JIMI

He told me . . . he told me this morning . . . before prayers that . . .

That that's it. It's over.

Poppy. The cunt I've fallen in love with.

It's a nickname. We've all got them.

I'm sorry. Forget it. I didn't mean to—

Well—he appeared about—six months ago—exactly six months ago—and we hit it off, just like that. I'd played around, as you do, even had a few girlfriends, but Poppy—well . . .

It was him started it all. He made the first move. We were doing a cross-country run, jogging along together, having a bit of a chat, and he suddenly stopped and said, 'Why don't you kiss me?', so I did, and from that moment to—to this morning, we haven't stopped.

He's kind of completely taken me over. It's been incredible; the best—the very best time of my life, and now . . .

It doesn't make sense. When he spoke to me today, there was nothing—nothing in his eyes—nothing to acknowledge what we'd . . . He's the only thing, Horace, that's meant anything. If that is it, then I don't see the point.

People always let you down, don't they? Give up on you, die on you, always fucking let you down.

Analysis: *The Day I Stood Still*

Type: Dramatic
Synopsis

Judy shows up unexpectedly on Horace's North London doorstep. They haven't seen each other in four years. Horace was best friends with Judy's husband, Jerry. Horace was, in fact, in love with Jerry. Once Jerry and Judy married, they saw Horace less and less frequently. Jerry died unexpectedly of blood poisoning when he cut himself on a piece of metal binding, reading Horace's manuscript.

Judy has arrived with her new French boyfriend, Guy. She has left her young son, Jimi, with his nanny. Horace is awaiting the arrival of a rent boy. Judy keeps calling the nanny to check on her son and finds out that he's missing. She and Guy run back to their hotel. Horace finds himself opening up to the rent boy but unable to sleep with him. They have an intense conversation, and then Horace is left alone.

The second scene jumps forward in time some twelve years. Jimi, now a young man, appears at Horace's door. He's run away from boarding school. Jimi is here because Horace knew his father. Jimi had a dream the night before and his father appeared to him. Jimi wanted to come here and find out more about Jerry. And so, Horace tells him about his Jerry. As the two men get drunk and high, Horace tells Jimi he used to have a chain of his father's but lost it a long time ago. Jimi's foot goes through a floorboard, uncovering the chain and closing the scene.

The final scene of the play flashes back thirty years to when Horace, Jerry, and Judy were seventeen. It's the last perfect day that Horace can remember.

Character Description
Jimi, 17 years old

His mother lives in Australia now, but he goes to boarding school in Hampshire. He's been in England for eighteen months. Jimi has run away from school. He thinks school is a waste of time. Judy thinks he's not motivated, merely drifting through life. Jimi was born with a big lump on his forehead that eventually went away, but he had no idea about it until Horace tells him. He does cocaine. He's looking for something to fight for, something to believe in.

Given Circumstances
Who are they? Horace is Jimi's godfather, but they've never met.
Where are they? Horace's apartment.
When does this take place? The late 1990s.
Why are they there? Jimi has run away from boarding school.
What is the pre-beat? Horace tells Jimi he thought he was his father.

Questions
1. Can you state your objective in a simple, specific, and active way?
2. Whom are you talking to? Be specific and have a clear image.
3. Can you think of three adjectives to describe your character?
4. How did you find Horace?
5. How much do you know about him before you get here?
6. Other than the picture you have of him from the 1960s, is this what you expected him to look like?
7. What would you like Horace to tell you about your father?
8. How much exactly do you know about your dad?
9. Do you like your mother? Do you miss her?
10. Why couldn't you tell her about your broken heart?
11. Is this the first time you've been in love?
12. Where do you feel the love in your body?

13. Where do you feel the pain of heartbreak?
14. What does Poppy look like?
15. How intimate has your relationship with him been?

Burnt Orange
Lila Feinberg

HUNTER

I used to come up here all the time. With my brother. We used
to smoke up here.

It was nice . . . before he got into harder stuff. Coke, meth,
heroin . . . then it wasn't so nice anymore.

He was a funny kid though. I remember once he got caught
in school with a ziplock bag of some substance, and he claimed
it was a prescription for the weight-loss substance Dexadrine.
Here was this little scrawny kid explaining to the Dean of Bronx
Science that childhood obesity was an epidemic caused by the
vending machines in the school, and Dexadrine was the only
way he could avoid becoming a victim of the cafeteria.

Yeah. And it was a nightmare too, cuz after he died, all these
kids wanted to make this memorial mural in the school, of all
his graffiti images. And I remember there was this one letter to
the editor published in the *New York Sun*, objecting to the whole
thing, saying that it was wrong "if these students succeed in hon-
oring and glorifying Nathaniel's illegal, criminal and destructive
graffiti artistry."

So, the mural was never built . . .

And now it's like every day is my mother and those boxes and
then you show up, and you're the first person to go into his room,
and everything feels different even though underneath nothing
has changed. I'm still *living here*.

Analysis: *Burnt Orange*

Type: Dramatic
Synopsis

The play takes place in a doorman building on the Upper East Side. Avery shows up with a mountain of baggage. She's not moving in, she's "migrating" to Jane's apartment and greeted, unexpectedly, by Hunter, Jane's son. Apparently Jane has sublet his room without letting him know. Avery has already paid $1,000 for the month, so she has to stay; that was all the money she had.

While Avery gets the rest of her stuff, Hunter confronts his mother. She says they need the money and he promised he was going to return to school this year. Hunter asks why she didn't ask his father for money, and Jane explains that his new wife won't allow it now that they are expecting a baby. Avery finds some journals and newspaper clippings in a drawer that pique her interest.

Harrison, Avery's hedge-fund nonboyfriend, wants to spend more time with her, but he's picked up cues from her that say "back off." He's set up an oxygen-controlled tent in his bedroom. Avery has a panic attack in the tent during sex and leaves.

Avery has a dream about Nate, Jane's young son who's in the journals and the clippings. She wakes up when her bed collapses. Hunter helps her screw the bed together. He asks Avery if she ever gets sick of playing some role—something she thinks she should be. Avery answers, "No that's the thing—I think we only ever get sick of playing ourselves." Hunter tells Avery that the room she's staying in used to be his brother Nate's. Hunter found him dead at fifteen. Avery gathers her stuff and goes even though Hunter insists that she stay.

Avery's mom has a serious accident. After spending a week in the hospital with her mother, Avery returns to the apartment. The ghost of Nate begins appearing to Avery, not just in dreams but all the time. Avery breaks up with Harrison, makes peace with Hunter, and goes off into the world; maybe she goes home for once.

Character Description
Hunter, late teens
Hunter dresses the part of the hipster who hates hipsters—tight old T-shirt, ripped jeans, grungy-sexy. He has a cutting sense of humor. He doesn't show much emotion in general and still carries the death of his brother like a weight around his neck. He has no idea Avery is moving in. He's not very welcoming to her when she arrives, or in general for the first few weeks. He promised his mom he would go back to college this semester, but he still hasn't returned. He can be angsty and aggressive, but underneath it all his heart is broken.

Given Circumstances
Who are they? Hunter is with Avery, whom he's known for about four weeks.
Where are they? The roof of Hunter's apartment building in Manhattan.
When does this take place? The present.
Why are they there? Avery has just ended a long, not terribly healthy relationship.
What is the pre-beat? They were just talking about the guy Avery broke up with.

Questions
1. Can you state your objective in a simple, specific, and active way?
2. Whom are you talking to? Be specific and have a clear image.
3. Can you think of three adjectives to describe your character?
4. What does Avery look like?
5. Are you attracted to her?

6. What does being up on the roof at night feel like?

7. What does the view look like from up here?

8. What did your brother, Nate, look like?

9. Where do you feel him in your body when you think of him?

10. What's your favorite memory of him?

11. You've been pretty mean to Avery the past few weeks. Why open up now?

12. Why haven't you gone back to college yet?

13. Where do you go to school?

14. What are you majoring in?

15. Where's the urgency in this monologue?

Baby Girl
Edith Freni

RICHIE

You got no cash, you got no place to live and your white knight
fancy food faggot up and left you just like all the others who came
before him present company included.

Yeah. I got locked up but—NEWSFLASH! I was leaving
anyway. And now that he's gone, it's gonna be you, El. Alone.
With a baby. Cuz history repeats. You wanna end up like your
mother? Tumor ridden? Yellow? Bankrupt? Begging for death
at the ripe old age of 52? You wanna raise another version of
yourself? Not very fair to that baby is it? Not when the potential
exists for her to have a real life. A REAL family. A family that can
provide.

And it's not very fair to you either. Or me. Cuz see, I wanna
make something of myself. Experience the American dream like
I'm entitled. Why all these towel-heads get to come over here
and live the high life and meanwhile I'm stuck in the fucking
mud? Doesn't sound fair to me, does that sound fair to you? Uh
uh. No. You know what you need, if you want those things?
Money. You know what that kid isn't going to make you? Money.
You know what you're going to spend on her for the next two
decades? You guessed it, MONEY. Money you don't have. Money
you'll never have.

Analysis: *Baby Girl*

Type: Dramatic
Synopsis

The play begins with Elise, our main character, in a restaurant kitchen asking Patrick for a job. She's recently been accused by her employer of stealing pills and, subsequently, fired. She desperately needs a job because she's a new mother. Patrick is her ex. He rebuffs her physical and emotional advances and sends her off with $100.

Richie is the father of Elise's baby and they came to a mutual decision that he wouldn't be a part of the baby's life but, of course, here he is. Elise hasn't named the baby girl yet, but she has given her Richie's last name, Higgins. Richie's solution to the financial problem is for Elise to sell the baby, and the two of them can split the money. Elise hates this idea and goes to Jason Higgins, her ex and Richie's brother. Jason will help Elise in exchange for sex or a date. Sensing no answer, Elise breaks down and finds herself at the motel where Richie stays, considering the option of selling Baby Girl.

Elise is a master of sexual and emotional manipulation, and she tries to seduce Richie again, but he calls her out on it, saying she coerced him into sleeping with her the first time, when he had no interest. Richie has other things on his mind—he's transitioning and having difficulties with the process.

A lawyer comes over and Elise asks many questions about what will happen to Baby Girl, where she'll end up, whom she'll end up with, et cetera. She figures out this lawyer, named Kush, is actually Richie's lover and they're planning on keeping Baby Girl for themselves. Elise gets locked up for stealing drugs, and Richie and Kush take Baby Girl. Patrick comes to the rescue, saying he'll help Elise find them.

Character Description

Richie, late teens

Richie is the father of Elise's baby, a petty thief, a repeat offender, and a pretty boy.

He's an emotional switchblade: quick, sharp, and dangerous. He's been following Elise, checking up on her and the baby. He feels like he has nothing to lose anymore.

Richie is also a pre-operative transsexual. He recently gave a woman a lot of money for silicone breast implants, but she only gave him one and it's rupturing and leaking into his body. He wants to raise Baby Girl with Kush, his lawyer boyfriend.

Given Circumstances

Who are they? Elise is Richie's former girlfriend and the mother of his baby.

Where are they? An empty Queens parking lot at night.

When does this take place? The present.

Why are they there? Richie has been following Elise. Start here

What is the pre-beat? Richie just called Elise out on being unemployed.

Questions

1. Can you state your objective in a simple, specific, and active way?
2. Whom are you talking to? Be specific and have a clear image.
3. Can you think of three adjectives to describe your character?
4. What does Elise look like?
5. How has she changed since you were dating?
6. How long did you date?
7. Are you still attracted to her at all?
8. How long have you been following her?
9. Have you met your baby yet?
10. Why do you think you'd be a better parent than Elise?

11. Why don't you tell her about your new boyfriend?
12. What do you do to make money?
13. How much does Kush support you?
14. Where do you live?
15. Where are you going to raise the baby?

How We Got On
Idris Goodwin

HANK

What up! Yeah, this is the microphone Mafioso comin' straight out The Hill! Got that new album coming real soon. Dope lyrics, fresh beats—Yeah!

Glad to finally be on *YO! MTV Raps!* I watch it all the time. I know usually you got rappers from New York and Compton, but I do my thing too. I mean, I got the skills to pay the bills— I'm fresher than anybody. Where I come from doesn't matter! It's about how I get busy on the mic. That's all that matters, right?

My parents' music is all R&B, "Baby come close! Let me do this! Why you leave me? Why won't you come back?" Sometimes that's how you feel. I guess.

Because everybody, well, most people in real life. They take an "L." Rich People. Poor. Handsome people. Ugly. Citizens. Immigrants. Everybody takes a loss. But in a rap song—you're the winner, even if you're small, you're fat, even if you're black and you live in The Hill.

No. Not a lot of black kids in The Hill. I stand out, sure. But not just cuz of that. Because I can rap. Oh yeah, they like rap out here, sure.

Not really though. As a joke I think. Even the other black kids say it's ghetto. They're all so stuck up. Everybody out here listens to like Rick Astley, INXS, Debbie Gibson.

But they know. Even if they don't like rap, they love rap. Or at least they will. Everybody will.

Anybody else?

There is NO competition. All the real good MCs live back in The City. But as far as The Hill. I am the fresh prince.

Analysis: *How We Got On*

Type: Seriocomic
Synopsis

"Hip Hop is body/toasting is the spirit.

Hip Hop culture is 15 years old/Rap music—younger—but it's on the move."

The play takes place over the summer of 1988 in Middle America, in a town that feels like nowhere.

Hank and Julian go to different schools, but both fancy themselves the "fresh prince" of The Hill. "Fresh Prince" is a reference to rapper/actor Will Smith and his popular sitcom *The Fresh Prince of Bel Air*. Hank is hungry for success. He challenges Julian to a rap-off, because there can't be two rappers on The Hill. It turns out that the two boys went to the same basketball camp together several years ago, but once they were put on separate teams they never spoke again.

A character called "The Selector" appears throughout the play. She serves many purposes, and in this instance she explains the rules and techniques necessary to win the rap battle: metaphor, simile, hyperbole, and alliteration. The unspoken rule is that it's better to go second in the battle because people will remember you. This battle takes place in the mall parking lot.

Julian, who's not quite as serious about all of this as Hank, wins the battle and takes off on Hank's bike. Hank finds him at work a few days later. He asks for his bike back, and Julian asks Hank to write rhymes for him. Julian has a better performance personality, and Hank has more precision with words. The Battle of the Bands is coming up, and Julian wants to win. Hank agrees, but they end up losing. Hank's words are almost too smart.

The boys buy recording equipment and begin making and passing out cheap records. They also spend a lot of time fighting over songwriting. Hanks finally breaks and punches Julian, storming out. This break causes him to find real inspiration, and he finally writes a truly great rap.

Meanwhile, Luann finds their demo at a grocery store and finds the boys, asking if she can rap with them. She feels as stuck on The Hill as the two boys do.

Hank's father threatens to take away the recording equipment, until he finally hears a rap and begins to understand it as a kind of poetry.

Character Description
Hank, 15 years old

His full name is Henry Charles, and he calls himself John Henry. Everyone calls him Hank. He's a high school freshman. He lives in The Hill, a suburb of a city some thirty-five miles away. He stands out from the other kids in his school and neighborhood, not just because he's black, but because he raps. He watches *Yo! MTV Raps* every day. He likes ham-and-pineapple pizza. His dream is to write the greatest suburban rap song.

Given Circumstances

Who are they? Hank is talking to The Selector (in his imagination).

Where are they? The suburban Midwest.

When does this take place? The summer of 1988.

Why are they there? Hank's dad moved the family there from The City.

What is the pre-beat? This is our first introduction to Hank.

Questions

1. Can you state your objective in a simple, specific, and active way?
2. Whom are you talking to? Be specific and have a clear image.
3. Can you think of three adjectives to describe your character?
4. Why do you love rap so much?
5. What do you feel like when you're creating rhymes?
6. What was life in The City like?
7. Did you have a lot of friends there?
8. How is life in the suburbs different?
9. How many friends do you have here?
10. Who are your biggest musical influences?
11. Do you listen to anything besides rap? What?
12. Are you a good student?
13. Do you show your raps to your parents?
14. What's your parents' financial status?
15. What's the urgency in this monologue?

How We Got On
Idris Goodwin

HANK

Tonight, I waited until the house was sleeping. I tiptoed down the steps. Got my bike. Needed a little fresh air. Some inspiration.

See, there is this water tower—probably the highest point really in The Hill. I remember when we moved out here from The City—I could see it from the freeway. I'd never seen anything like it.

I always imagined that on the top you could probably see the whole town, that you could get in touch, channel all the creativity flowing. But every time I go there, I look at how high to the top and realize—I'm not as brave as I think.

And then it started to rain, but I stayed. I sat underneath the water tower. Listened to the rain. I knew there was something better. I just had to wait for it.

Shut my eyes tight, waited. And then something better came.

Straight off the interstate/no skyscrapers
Far from the street talk and sky pagers
Far from the corners/graffiti/street lights
car speakers bumpin' jams that we like
The Hill/we straight from The Hill
But this is where we chill/yeah right here
Green in The Hill
quiet in The Hill
But listen right here
There's a riot in The Hill

Analysis: *How We Got On*

Type: Dramatic
Synopsis
"Hip Hop is body/toasting is the spirit.
Hip Hop culture is 15 years old/Rap music—younger—but it's on the move."

The play takes place over the summer of 1988 in Middle America, in a town that feels like nowhere.

Hank and Julian go to different schools, but both fancy themselves the "fresh prince" of The Hill. "Fresh Prince" is a reference to rapper/actor Will Smith and his popular sitcom *The Fresh Prince of Bel Air*. Hank is hungry for success. He challenges Julian to a rap-off, because there can't be two rappers on The Hill. It turns out that the two boys went to the same basketball camp together several years ago, but once they were put on separate teams they never spoke again.

A character called "The Selector" appears throughout the play. She serves many purposes, and in this instance she explains the rules and techniques necessary to win the rap battle: metaphor, simile, hyperbole, and alliteration. The unspoken rule is that it's better to go second in the battle because people will remember you. This battle takes place in the mall parking lot.

Julian, who's not quite as serious about all of this as Hank, wins the battle and takes off on Hank's bike. Hank finds him at work a few days later. He asks for his bike back, and Julian asks Hank to write rhymes for him. Julian has a better performance personality, and Hank has more precision with words. A battle of the bands is coming up, and Julian wants to win. Hank agrees, but they end up losing. Hank's words are almost too smart.

The boys buy recording equipment and begin making and passing out cheap records. They also spend a lot of time fighting over songwriting. Hanks finally breaks and punches Julian, storming out. This break causes him to find real inspiration, and he finally writes a truly great rap.

Meanwhile, Luann finds their demo at a grocery store and finds the boys, asking if she can rap with them. She feels as stuck on The Hill as the two boys do.

Hank's father threatens to take away the recording equipment, until he finally hears a rap and begins to understand it as a kind of poetry.

Character Description
Hank, 15 years old
His full name is Henry Charles, and he calls himself John Henry. Everyone calls him Hank. He's a high school freshman. He lives in The Hill, a suburb of a city some thirty-five miles away. He stands out from the other kids in his school and neighborhood, not just because he's black, but because he raps. He watches *Yo! MTV Raps* every day. He likes ham-and-pineapple pizza. His dream is to write the greatest suburban rap song.

Given Circumstances
Who are they? Hank is talking to The Selector in his imagination.
Where are they? The suburban Midwest.
When does this take place? The summer of 1988.
Why are they there? Hank is looking for inspiration.
What is the pre-beat? Julian has just criticized Hank's recent rhymes.

Questions
1. Can you state your objective in a simple, specific, and active way?
2. Whom are you talking to? Be specific and have a clear image.
3. Can you think of three adjectives to describe your character?

4. How long have you and Julian been friends?
5. How does your working relationship function?
6. What does Julian look like?
7. How do you handle criticism?
8. How do you start writing a rap?
9. Where do you find inspiration?
10. What are the recurring themes in your raps?
11. What drives you to create music?
12. What is life in the suburbs like?
13. How is it different from life in The City?
14. Do your parents support your rap?
15. Do you show them your material?

How We Got On
Idris Goodwin

JULIAN

I don't take L's, I hand 'em out!

I should've won that. Those were some weird rhymes you gave me. What the hell is a "Can-tor." Nobody knows what a "Can-tor" is.

It's NOT okay. Losing is not allowed in my house!

What's your father do, Hank?

My father was like, All-American in football, basketball, track. He was the number one sales rep for the whole Midwest for like 5 years in a row. All my half-brothers are top-ranked in whatever they do. Nobody loses in my family, Hank! You might be satisfied to just be okay. But not me—not me!

Steel and Dan? Hells no. That rock stuff is wack. A lot of that stuff—that heavy metal, you can't even understand what they say. Not like you're missing anything. (*Imitating a metal lead singer.*) "Bat heads, swords, the end of the world!" And they say rap is bad. Least it ain't a horror movie.

I'm gonna get me an instrument. You'll write me some fresher rhymes. I'm gonna come back and show The Hill what's up. Show everybody.

Analysis: *How We Got On*

Type: Dramatic
Synopsis

The play takes place over the summer of 1988 in Middle America, in a town that feels like nowhere.

Hank and Julian go to different schools, but both fancy themselves the "fresh prince" of The Hill. "Fresh Prince" is a reference to rapper/actor Will Smith and his popular sitcom *The Fresh Prince of Bel Air*. Hank is hungry for success. He challenges Julian to a rap-off, because there can't be two rappers on The Hill. It turns out that the two boys went to the same basketball camp together several years ago, but once they were put on separate teams they never spoke again.

A character called "The Selector" appears throughout the play. She serves many purposes, and in this instance she explains the rules and techniques necessary to win the rap battle: metaphor, simile, hyperbole, and alliteration. The unspoken rule is that it's better to go second in the battle because people will remember you. This battle takes place in the mall parking lot.

Julian, who's not quite as serious about all of this as Hank, wins the battle and takes off on Hank's bike. Hank finds him at work a few days later. He asks for his bike back, and Julian asks Hank to write rhymes for him. Julian has a better performance personality, and Hank has more precision with words. A battle of the bands is coming up, and Julian wants to win. Hank agrees, but they end up losing. Hank's words are almost too smart.

The boys buy recording equipment and begin making and passing out cheap records. They also spend a lot of time fighting over songwriting. Hanks finally breaks and punches Julian, storming out. This break causes him to find real inspiration, and he finally writes a truly great rap.

Meanwhile, Luann finds their demo at a grocery store and finds the boys, asking if she can rap with them. She feels as stuck on The Hill as the two boys do.

Hank's father threatens to take away the recording equipment, until he finally hears a rap and begins to understand it as a kind of poetry.

Character Description
Julian, 15 years old
Julian's full name is Julian Mark Hayes. He refers to himself as any of the following: the rhyme villain, the lyrical criminal, or the smooth soul technician. His rap name is Vic Vicious. He shows up fifteen minutes late for the rap battle with Hank, wearing new Jordans. He's a crystal-clean rapper whose smooth style makes it look easy and cool. Julian knows he performs better than Hank, while recognizing Hank may be better with words, so he asks Hank to ghostwrite for him.

He attends Hill Foster High. He likes to beatbox and wants to learn drums. He's very resistant to Luanne being in the group, because he fears she's better than both Hank and himself.

Given Circumstances
Who are they? Julian and Hank have only recently met and started working together.
Where are they? The suburban Midwest.
When does this take place? The summer of 1988.
Why are they there? Julian has just performed at the Battle of the Bands.
What is the pre-beat? Julian just learned he didn't even place in the top three.

Questions
1. Can you state your objective in a simple, specific, and active way?
2. Who are you talking to? Be specific and have a clear image.

3. Can you think of three adjectives to describe your character?
4. What did it feel like to perform in the Battle of the Bands?
5. Were you happy with your performance?
6. How did it feel to lose?
7. How do you and Hank function as a rap-writing team?
8. How long have you been working together?
9. What does Hank look like?
10. Do you guys get along?
11. What do your parents think about your rapping?
12. How much input do you have in the songwriting?
13. Do your parents support your rapping?
14. Have they heard your rapping?
15. What's life in suburbia like?

The Tutor
Allan Havis

ORSON

Tucker wrote a cool short story on MySpace. About the murder of Alexis Trachenberg. Really had great style and rhythm. A bio-chem death in the high school science lab. Did a great job in PhotoShop with the illustrations. Tucker thought it cool to attack every Trachenberg orifice with a toxic substance. And she got sick the next week after he posted the story. You see, Tucker really likes Dario Argento films. Italian Hitchcock with a twisted touch.

But you could really appreciate this if you knew Alexis. She's such a cow. Like no other mad cow in the world. She walks around top heavy like she's carrying three bazooka tits. And she's got this dumb Jewish smile that drives me insane. You know the face, on the dumb balloon cartoons at the mall, and that backside of hers is bigger than a fuck-ass Hummer.

Tucker tried to mount her once, but he couldn't get hard to save his life.

My Dad can't stand Tucker and I kind of love that. My Mom lets Tucker come to the house just to piss off my Dad. I kind of love that too. She just lets us get high if it's the weekend. So you got to give her credit sometimes.

I'd love to get high with you, Mr. Kane, but that shouldn't surprise you. My Mom is an only child, you see. And that's why she needs to be part of the scene.

We both want you intensely.

Analysis: *The Tutor*

Type: Seriocomic
Synopsis

The play opens with the very first tutoring session between Seth Kane, the tutor, and Orson Bentley. Seth has been hired to help Orson with his work in English class. The first novel on their list to discuss is *The Great Gatsby* by F. Scott Fitzgerald. Orson is aggressive, reactive, and assaultive. He tries desperately to get a rise out of his new tutor. Seth deftly handles everything Orson throws at him.

Seth prefers working with troubled teens. Currently, he teaches in the public school system. Orson's father is a skilled businessman and has negotiated Seth's fee for this down to a pittance. Mr. Bentley has also revealed to Seth that he and his wife are on a trial separation and he is already seeing someone in his office because he needs "magic" in his life. Seth finds himself on the receiving end of Mrs. Bentley's depression and sexual advances. In fact, the entire family seems to be taking advantage of him in one way or another.

Despite the tension and dysfunction, Seth keeps returning. His relationship with Orson seems to be developing and helping the boy. The Bentley house is broken into, and pieces from Mr. Bentley's gun collection go missing. Seth speaks with a young woman claiming to be Orson's girlfriend. She says that she is pregnant with Orson's baby and that he is obsessed with Columbine, feeling a kinship with Dylan Klebold, one of the gunmen. Seth presses Orson to admit whether or not he's planning a school shooting, but Orson is so coy and such a skilled liar that Seth can't decipher fact from fiction.

Orson and Tucker, his best friend, kidnap someone from school. Orson calls Seth and asks him to come and take him home. It turns out that Orson acted alone. There is no Tucker. Orson crafted the entire scenario. When Seth discovers this, he terminates his relationship with

Orson and then mysteriously ends up in the hospital in a coma. Was Orson the cause of this?

Character Description
Orson Bentley, 16 years old

Orson is sullen, wealthy, a delinquent and a cigarette smoker. He appears to be a strong writer who reminds Seth of a young Hemingway mixed with Hunter S. Thompson. He has a pet python, named "W" in a patriotic reference to President George W. Bush. Orson hates his father. He does not like to be touched. His IQ is over 170. His driver's license was taken away because of a hit-and-run that he says his dad covered up by paying off the cops.

Orson has been through nine tutors so far. He keeps gun magazines under his bed. Mrs. Bentley claims he is afraid of girls. He reads Camus, Sartre, and underground political journals.

Given Circumstances
Who are they? Seth is Orson's new tutor.

Where are they? The living room of the Bentleys' Southern California house.

When does this take place? 2006.

Why are they there? Seth has been tutoring Orson for a few weeks.

What is the pre-beat? Seth just asked if Orson and his friend Tucker have firearms.

Questions
1. Can you state your objective in a simple, specific, and active way?
2. Whom are you talking to? Be specific and have a clear image.
3. Can you think of three adjectives to describe your character?
4. What does Seth look like?
5. How long has he been tutoring you?

6. Why do you need a tutor?

7. How dysfunctional is your home life?

8. What are your feelings on your mom and dad?

9. How do you know about Dario Argento, Mario Bava, and Alfred Hitchcock?

10. How rich is your dad?

11. How does having money affect your relationship with Seth, who has little?

12. Can you describe Tucker?

13. What does your room look like?

14. What do you find attractive about Seth?

15. Is it difficult or easy to tell him you're attracted?

The Tutor
Allan Havis

ORSON

Happy birthday, Daddy! I remembered.

Here's something for you. I want you to open it. Yeah, and the card's inside.

How old is the old man today? Okay. I don't need to know your age. But I think you're a fag, Daddy. And you have a wide stance at the urinal and at the toilet stall. I notice these things because I've got a sharp eye.

My gift to you? A silk blouse from Nordstrom's. Couple of hundred bucks. Yep. That's all Mom talked about last week. An imported blouse from Italy. But she was in on you. It's your favorite color, Daddy. Robin's egg blue. And you know I'm color blind.

I know you've embezzled a shitload of money from the corporation. Maybe the cops will never know because you know how to play the cops. And I know little Phyllis has you eating from a doggy bowl. And Mom is a million times superior to this little cunt Phyllis. And I know Jesus is smiling down on us right now 'cause Jesus knows I am capable of doing great historic deeds. Aren't we all searching for our beautiful reward, Daddy?

Reward and a whisper.

Analysis: *The Tutor*

Type: Seriocomic
Synopsis

The play opens with the very first tutoring session between Seth Kane, the tutor, and Orson Bentley. Seth has been hired to help Orson with his work in English class. The first novel on their list to discuss is *The Great Gatsby* by F. Scott Fitzgerald. Orson is aggressive, reactive, and assaultive. He tries desperately to get a rise out of his new tutor. Seth deftly handles everything Orson throws at him.

Seth prefers working with troubled teens. Currently, he teaches in the public school system. Orson's father is a skilled businessman and has negotiated Seth's fee for this down to a pittance. Mr. Bentley has also revealed to Seth that he and his wife are on a trial separation and he is already seeing someone in his office because he needs "magic" in his life. Seth finds himself on the receiving end of Mrs. Bentley's depression and sexual advances. In fact, the entire family seems to be taking advantage of him in one way or another.

Despite the tension and dysfunction, Seth keeps returning. His relationship with Orson seems to be developing and helping the boy. The Bentley house is broken into, and pieces from Mr. Bentley's gun collection go missing. Seth speaks with a young woman claiming to be Orson's girlfriend. She says that she is pregnant with Orson's baby and that he is obsessed with Columbine, feeling a kinship with Dylan Klebold, one of the gunmen. Seth presses Orson to admit whether or not he's planning a school shooting, but Orson is so coy and such a skilled liar that Seth can't decipher fact from fiction.

Orson and Tucker, his best friend, kidnap someone from school. Orson calls Seth and asks him to come and take him home. It turns out that Orson acted alone. There is no Tucker. Orson crafted the entire scenario. When Seth discovers this, he terminates his relationship with

Orson and then mysteriously ends up in the hospital in a coma. Was Orson the cause of this?

Character Description
Orson Bentley, 16 years old
Orson is sullen, wealthy, a delinquent and a cigarette smoker. He appears to be a strong writer who reminds Seth of a young Hemingway mixed with Hunter S. Thompson. He has a pet python, named "W" in a patriotic reference to President George W. Bush. Orson hates his father. He does not like to be touched. His IQ is over 170. His driver's license was taken away because of a hit-and-run that he says his dad covered up by paying off the cops.

Orson has been through nine tutors so far. He keeps gun magazines under his bed. Mrs. Bentley claims he is afraid of girls. He reads Camus, Sartre, and underground political journals.

Given Circumstances
Who are they? Orson is talking to his father.
Where are they? The Bentleys' house in Southern California.
When does this take place? 2006.
Why are they there? It's Mr. Bentley's birthday.
What is the pre-beat? This is the top of the scene.

Questions
1. Can you state your objective in a simple, specific, and active way?
2. Whom are you talking to? Be specific and have a clear image.
3. Can you think of three adjectives to describe your character?
4. Do you always call your father "Daddy"?
5. What does your father look like?
6. Do you resemble him?
7. What's the relationship between your mother and father like?

8. Is this interaction typical of your relationship with your father?

9. What does being gay mean to you?

10. Would you ever tell your father that you have feelings for your tutor?

11. How rich is your family?

12. What is your father's business?

13. Does it bother you that your father is having an affair?

14. Do you believe in God/Jesus/religion?

15. What's the urgency behind this monologue?

The Greatest Show on Earth
Michael Kimmel

JOSEF

I am not in any physical danger. I have not been forbidden from coming home. I am sixteen and I wish to live away from home. And yes, I manage my own finances. These are the only qualifications for emancipation, yes?

My parents are Sascha and Svetlana Schmitt. Address is . . . complicated. They travel around. A lot. It's a big reason for my emancipation. They perform in Frederick Sparks's Big Top 3-Ring Circus, Animal Emporium and House of Wonderment. They are trapeze artists. They do not know I am here. They would probably not allow it. My sister, Kata, and I have never been away from them. Kata? She is very happy at the circus. She is a performer there. I don't have the . . . skill sets the rest of my family possesses. I tried for a long time to be a trapeze artist, but . . .

I didn't attend a school. I was home schooled, and passed my GED two years ago. I would like to go to college, but my parents have different ideas. I don't want to move away again. My father was injured two months ago, and we stayed here in this town while he recuperated. It was the longest we have ever stayed in one place. I like it here, and would like to be settled before I apply to colleges.

My finances come from the job I have held for the last 5 years. When I found out that I was not going to perform with my family, I needed to do something else for the show — everyone earns their keep in the Circus. Mr. Sparks, owner and ringmaster, had an opening in the office keeping the finances straight. He paid me a fair sum that I have saved and invested. I have just put a down payment on an apartment in town, and secured a job with a local CPA.

Thank you. It doesn't feel impressive or grown up. I have always been somewhat of a disappointment to my family, and this will only make it worse. Not that they have ever said anything to me, but you could see my father's heart break when I couldn't catch the trapeze. I practiced over and over, hundreds of hours. I have always been good with numbers, and I like the work. I wish more than anything to become a registered accountant, with a home, a dog and a normal life. I cannot have this living with a circus.

Listens.

(*Sigh*) . . . Yes. I am sure you are right. This is probably the first time anyone has run away from the circus. But I don't think it's that amusing.

Analysis: *The Greatest Show on Earth*

Type: Seriocomic
Synopsis and Character Description

This piece was written as a stand-alone monologue, so all of the factual information you need about the character and events can be found within.

The character's name is Josef, and he is sixteen years old. He lives away from home. He is looking to emancipate himself from his parents, which means he must be at some sort of government or legal office. He is under no threat or danger from his parents. They do not know he is here. Josef manages his own finances.

The spelling of Josef's name and the way he uses language lead one to believe that he perhaps was born in a country other than America. He has spent most of his sixteen years traveling the world with his parents, who are trapeze artists in Frederick Sparks' Big Top 3-Ring Circus, Animal Emporium and House of Wonderment. His sister has inherited the family performance gene, whereas Josef's skills lean more toward finances and mathematics.

Josef must be fairly bright to have achieved his GED by the age of sixteen. He's anxious to continue with his education, as he is already considering applying to college. After a lifetime of travel, two months in this town must have felt like a blessing for someone searching for stability.

By the age of eleven it was clear that Josef could not perform trapeze. It is true that everyone in the circus has to support the group, so it's interesting that also by the age of eleven Josef discovered what his skills and passion were.

Wherever this town is, Josef must have been putting quite a lot of money aside in savings and investments to be able to afford a down payment on an apartment for himself. His dream is in place, and he is going to make it happen no matter what.

Be cautious of judging Josef. His dream of settling down to a normal life and finding a job as a CPA isn't any less interesting or difficult than being an actor or writer or artist. It is his dream, and if you're going to perform this monologue, you must endow it with the same passion and no judgment.

Given Circumstances
Who are they? Josef is talking to a government official.
Where are they? A sterile government office.
When does this take place? The present.

Why are they there? Josef is seeking emancipation from his parents.
What is the pre-beat? The official has asked Josef if he's in any danger or under any threat.

Questions

1. Can you state your objective in a simple, specific, and active way?
2. Whom are you talking to? Be specific and have a clear image.
3. Can you think of three adjectives to describe your character?
4. What state is this taking place in?
5. How long have you been on a break from touring?
6. What does this official look like? (Is it a man or a woman?)
7. How long have you been planning this?
8. What is life in the circus like?
9. Is there any part of it that you enjoy?
10. What does it feel like when you're working with numbers?
11. Can you describe your parents?
12. Do you love them?
13. How long have you been planning this emancipation?
14. Have you told anyone else about it?
15. What do you imagine your future to look like when you think about it?

Henry's Law
Stacie Lents

JASON

Your phone works.

I've been texting you.

I texted you fifteen times during Algebra; I texted you twenty-six times during French; I texted you thirty-two times during wrestling and now Coach is threatening to pull me from the match tomorrow after I stopped eating for three days to make weight. I'm friggin' starving.

I was WORRIED, Sara! I couldn't find you during study period. I looked everywhere.

You think you're so friggin' smart all of a sudden, Sara. Ignoring me every time I wanna hang out, like everyone's gonna stop breathing tomorrow if you don't memorize the goddamn formula for air. But you know what, Sara? Most people at this school don't give a crap about H_2O unless they're skinny-dipping in it. And guess what? You're most people. I mean I can't believe I bought all that bull about you and Mad Max going around talking about gravity this and pressure that. What a load of crap.

You want pressure? I'll give you pressure.

Max was right. You are just a tease.

Analysis: *Henry's Law*

Type: Dramatic
Synopsis

Max and Annie are siblings. Max, about seventeen years old, is the older brother. He's far from cool. In fact, he's kind of a science nerd. He conducts experiments in his bedroom. Annie, fifteen years old and a freshman, wants to be popular and isn't exactly proud about living in her older brother's geeky shadow. In the first scene, we learn that Max is preparing to tutor Sara Culverson, a popular kid and the girlfriend of Jason Swarthmore. Annie, who has been trying to teach him how to flirt, tells him that flirting is in fact useless with Sara because she's out of his league.

The first tutoring session takes place in Sara's bedroom, and it's awkward. Max misidentifies an Usher poster as Justin Bieber and is just generally awkward. But the two finally find some common ground and get to work.

Sara comes to Max's house for another study session. After Annie does a lengthy photo shoot with Sara for her Facebook page, Max and Annie get to talking. Sara finds herself attracted to Max and kisses him. Annie walks in and sees this. The next day at school, Annie finds Jason and tells him she saw Sara kissing another boy. Jason loses it.

An online viral smear campaign against Max, falsely outing him as a homosexual, begins. It seems like Jason is the one behind it. Annie is most worried about how the scandal will affect her.

Max stops returning Sara's calls and even stops going to school. Max kills himself. He purchases arsenic online and takes it. Jason is ostracized at school. Everyone blames him for Max's suicide. When he goes to Sara for comfort, she admits that she was the one who started the online rumors because Max wouldn't respond to her advances.

Character Description
Jason Swarthmore, 17–18 years old
Jason is a somewhat intense guy. He favors a casual outfit of T-shirt, jeans, and a baseball cap. When he hangs out in Sara's room he'll send her text messages to get her attention. He'll even call her from another room for her help to find something in the kitchen. He gets upset when Sara corrects his use of language: he says "anterior" instead of "ulterior" in a sentence. Jason drinks Sara's dad's beers from the fridge. Jason refers to Max as "Mad Max" and even as a "little faggot." He manipulates Sara, emotionally and physically, into not doing her homework.

Given Circumstances
Who are they? Sara and Jason have been a couple for a while now.
Where are they? Outside Clearview High School.
When does this take place? The present.
Why are they there? Jason has been standing there waiting for her.
What is the pre-beat? Jason has walked right up to Sara, who didn't see him because she was texting.

Questions
1. Can you state your objective in a simple, specific, and active way?
2. Whom are you talking to? Be specific and have a clear image.
3. Can you think of three adjectives to describe your character?
4. How long have you and Sara been a couple?
5. What does she look like?
6. Are you in love with her?
7. Have you ever cheated on her?
8. Annie told you Max kissed Sara. How did that information hit you?
9. What does Max look like?
10. Max is a nerd. Have you ever had a conversation with him?
11. How many texts have you sent Sara?

12. When did you start texting?
13. How long have you been waiting outside for her?
14. Can you look at Sara without imagining Max's lips on hers?
15. What could she say to you right now to make things better?

Snow Angel
David Lindsay-Abaire

ARLO

I went grocery shopping with my mother last week, and she put a box of tampons in the cart. They were right there for everyone to see, right on top of the Pop Tarts.

I pretended I didn't notice, but when we got to the checkout line, Dan Sherman was bagging. He's in my English class. He saw the tampons right away and smiled at me, real big, like they were my tampons. I pretended I didn't see him.

The next day, he stopped me in front of the lockers and said "Hey how'd those tampons work out for your old lady?" And I pretended I didn't hear him. So he said it again real loud, so everyone could hear. "Hey, how'd those tampons work out for your old lady?!"

And I said "Menstruation is a natural part of a woman's life cycle. I'm sure your mother menstruates too." And he turned red and said I shouldn't talk about his mother and I should shut my mouth.

And then he beat the hell out of me, but I pretended it didn't hurt.

Analysis: *Snow Angel*

Type: Seriocomic
Synopsis

The town of Deerpoint, Vermont, suffers its worst snowstorm in 107 years. As the kids sit around their radios listening for school closure announcements, the broadcaster reads the list in no particular order, even throwing in items on his grocery list to prolong the torture. Finally Deerpoint is announced, along with the information that class 301, Mrs. Sampson's class, should remember to write in their journals every day.

Lindsay-Abaire tells the story through short scenes as well as stylized moments in which the students read aloud to the audience from their journals. The action takes place over the course of the day, exploring the different social statuses, cliques, and crushes that develop in a typical American high school.

Frida Jensen, something of an outcast, is the first person to spot an unknown young girl named Eva making snow angels in a drift. Eva says that she's looking for Whitestone Farm. Apparently Catherine, Eva's younger sister, ran off from the farm and Eva went after her but now seems to have lost her way.

Frida works at the Pretzel Knot. Her classmates come in to hang out, after a harrowing car ride in the storm, and make fun of her for being different. Frida runs out the back, very upset, and once again Eva appears, telling Frida not to get so angry. When Frida runs out she leaves her journal behind and the other kids read it. They find out about Eva, and pretty soon every one of them claims to have seen of her all over town, some of the stories so ridiculous as to seem absurd.

At the library one or two of the students finds out that Eva matches the description of a young girl who disappeared on February 3, 1891 — exactly 107 years ago — under similar circumstances. Things get out of control and a prank goes horribly wrong, endangering the lives of many of them. The kids finally rally around Frida and accept her as part of the group, in part thanks to Eva.

Character Description
Arlo, early teens

Arlo is a somewhat wimpy kid just trying to get by without making waves. This monologue is an entry in his journal. He kind of likes Michael Bolton, the singer, but would never admit to it.

He's very smart and savvy. In fact, Arlo is the one who goes online at the library and finds the connection between Eva and the farm and the disappearance 107 years ago. However, he believes, at first, that Frida made up the story because she posted questions on an Internet forum about the story a week or so before the storm.

Given Circumstances

Who are they? Arlo is talking directly to the audience.

Where are they? Deerpoint, Vermont.

When does this take place? 1992.

Why are they there? There's a major snowstorm and school has been canceled.

What is the pre-beat? This is the beginning of the scene.

Questions

1. Can you state your objective in a simple, specific, and active way?
2. Whom are you talking to? Be specific and have a clear image. "The audience" isn't a good enough answer, so make it a single person, someone you can relate to.
3. Can you think of three adjectives to describe your character?
4. What does Dan Sherman look like?
5. Had you ever had an encounter with him before?

6. What does your mother look like?

7. What are the cliques at your school?

8. Do you have a particular group of friends?

9. Were you bullied your entire life?

10. Have you been beaten up before?

11. You're technically savvy; do you spend a lot of time online?

12. Are you going to leave this town as soon as you're old enough?

13. What do you want to be when you're older?

14. What are your hobbies?

15. What's the urgency behind this monologue?

Peddling
Harry Melling

BOY

good evening, miss.
and what a beautiful evening it is.
(i said) what a beautiful evening it is.
—

you may or may not already know this.
but i've come all this way, to find you today.
—

i swam through cement and long grass
just so's i could ask—
you one little thing.
(ha . . . .
and now—
look at me i'm shaking.)

you see . . .
nineteen years ago . . .
i was born . . .
and didn't grow.
—

nineteen years ago . . .
something happened—
and I still don't know quite what?
—

so i'm here today . . .

on this doorstep . . .
taking this first step
(whatever that
turns out to be?
it's all fine, i'm not bad.

—

let me start that again

—

(ha) . . .
so i'm today . . .
and i'm wondering . . .
wondering . . .
whether or not . . .
whether or not . . .
i've got a shot at . . .
(whether or not, i've got a shot)
at . . .
asking you . . .
whether or not . . .
whether or not . . .

you would like to buy something?

'here' we have the everyday essentials. some
might call life's essentials.'
'no thank you.' she says, closing the door on me.

Analysis: *Peddling*

Type: Dramatic
Synopsis

An unnamed Boy wakes up in a field surrounded by cigarette butts, beer cans, a backpack, and an orange plastic crate. He vomits three times.

Then he begins to recount a story that started three days ago. The Bossman drives Boy and some other young men in a "magic" white van. The boys — seven in all — do a job (selling stolen goods), and the Bossman collects money from them. Bossman puts pressure on them to make a lot of money. They go off and sell the merchandise door-to-door. Bossman calls them all while they're out peddling to speed them up. Their crates contain items such as toilet paper, oven mitts, toothpaste, and toothbrushes.

Boy comes across a woman who doesn't buy anything, but she feels for him and gives him a five. Boy thinks he recognizes her. In fact, he thinks she could be his mother. He spends a lot of time outside her house wondering what to do.

Bossman times all of these trips. Boy forgets to check his phone, and when he finally does he has six missed calls from Bossman. Bossman threatens to kill Boy for not showing up at the expected time with money.

Boy tries to hitchhike back, but no one will pick him up. He goes back to the woman's home with a firecracker. He thinks that he'll threaten to shoot her with it if she doesn't answer his question: Are you my mother?

Character Description
Boy, 17–19 years old

He has a hangover so bad that it feels like he's headbutting glass. The flicking of the streetlights is enough to hurt his eyes. Boy has no interest in getting to know the other boys in the van. He just wants to get on with the work, get his money, and get out of there. He has to wear a "young offender's ID." The orange crates filled with merchandise are strapped around their necks for convenience. He's often chided by neighborhood kids because he's an outsider.

Although Boy has a tough exterior, he has a heart and a conscience. When an old woman tried to buy his entire stash, he turns her down because he realizes that she is senile and he "ain't no thief." Boy hopes there's a light at the end of his road, an answer to all of the questions he's been fighting to answer his entire life.

Given Circumstances

Who are they? Harry is talking to a woman he thinks may be his mother.

Where are they? A residential section of London.

When does this take place? The present.

Why are they there? Harry is back at her door because he thought she seemed familiar.

What is the pre-beat? This is the beginning of the scene.

Questions

1. Can you state your objective in a simple, specific, and active way?
2. Whom are you talking to? Be specific and have a clear image.
3. Can you think of three adjectives to describe your character?
4. Where do you live?
5. Whom do you live with?
6. Do you have any other jobs besides this one?
7. How much money do you need to make per week in order to survive?
8. Are you involved in any other illegal activities?
9. When was the last time you saw your mother?

10. What did she look like?

11. What is it about this woman that reminds you of her?

12. Where do you feel her in your body?

13. What is the best thing she can say to you right now?

14. How long have you waited to knock on the door?

15. What's so urgent about this monologue?

Apocalypse Apartments
Allison Moore

MICK

Imagine it.

Patti Smith, Robert Mapplethorpe and Sam fucking Shepard, having a threesome. It happened. You know it happened.

You don't know who Robert Mapplethorpe is?

Okay, Robert Mapplethorpe was a photographer, a very famous photographer—The lilies? The giant lilies? Or the cover of Horses, right? The photo on the cover, Patti Smith, with the jacket and the tie and she's looking right in the camera with a face that's like—

All right, he was a photographer. And he and Patti Smith were best friends, they lived together—he was mostly gay, but sometimes, you know? And then Patti and Sam Shepard had some kinda crazy intense thing going at the same time. So it's like three geniuses, all together one night at the Chelsea Hotel, stoned out of their minds, radiating their genius-ness all over each other . . . ? You cannot tell me they didn't have a threesome.

And you can bet that Sam Shepard fucked the shit out of Robert Mapplethorpe. And then Patti strapped on her dildo and fucked 'em both. Oh my God she was hot. She was like a man she was so hot, you know what I mean? That aggressive, that unapologetic. She was a force. I mean, have you ever seen her perform?

It's unbelievable.

Analysis: *Apocalypse Apartments*

Type: Comedic
Synopsis

Apocalypse Apartments is a short play inside an evening of works commissioned by the Humana Festival's 2011 anthology exploring the end of the world.

Mick, Tyler, and Zoe are in Apartment 1A. Mick opens the play asking the other two to imagine Patti Smith, Robert Mapplethorpe, and Sam Shepard having a threesome.

Meanwhile, there is an apocalypse raging outside, and the three of them are in the apartment on lockdown. Zoe and Tyler are a couple. Tyler doesn't want to hear anything about this. He doesn't want anyone introducing the possibility of a threesome into his relationship, and he certainly doesn't want Zoe engaging, questioning, or encouraging Mick. Unfortunately, Zoe was listening to Patti Smith's song "Gloria" when the first wave of the apocalypse started.

Tyler is freaking out. He keeps re-sealing the windows and checking to see how much water from their supply has evaporated from the bathtub. Half the people they know are dead. They're not even sure if the Pacific Northwest exists anymore.

Zoe tries to comfort Tyler after his breakdown, but he rejects her. She sticks her hand down her pants and proceeds to masturbate. Mick follows suit. There is nothing particularly sexual between the two of them, but it kills the time. Tyler, furious, storms out.

Character Description
Mick, mid- to late teens
He thinks a lot about sex. He is completely oblivious to Zoe and Tyler fighting while he tells his story. He finds the idea of a threesome powerful and exciting. He finds nothing wrong in engaging in mutual

masturbation with Zoe even when there's nothing sexual between the two of them.

Given Circumstances

Who are they? Three friends locked in an apartment together.
Where are they? Apartment 1A in a large unnamed city.
When does this take place? The present.
Why are they there? There's an apocalypse happening outside.
What is the pre-beat? This piece opens the play.

Questions

1. Can you state your objective in a simple, specific, and active way?
2. Whom are you talking to? Be specific and have a clear image.
3. Can you think of three adjectives to describe your character?
4. Whose apartment is this?
5. What does it look like?
6. How long have you, Zoe, and Tyler known each other?
7. Have you ever had feelings for Zoe?
8. Are you proposing a threesome among you all?
9. What do they look like?
10. Are they a good couple together?
11. What is it about this story that turns you on most?
12. How big of a Patti Smith fan are you?
13. What do you want to do for a living?
14. What kind of apocalypse is happening outside?
15. What would the couple's ideal response to this story be?

Apocalypse Apartments
Allison Moore

MICK

Patti Smith? Oh my God she was hot. She was like a man she was so hot, you know what I mean? That aggressive, that unapologetic. She was a force. I mean, have you ever seen her perform?

I'm talking about footage, from back in the day

It's unbelievable. There's this clip I found online: she's on stage, with her hand down her pants, finger fucking herself, while she's singing. It's amazing. Sends chills down my spine just thinking about it. It's like: Fuck yeah! Choke on that Jack Johnson. Justin Bieber. Or fucking Fergie, shaking her ass for the camera.

Let me tell you something, Patti Smith was not putting on a show. She wasn't trying to sell anything, she wasn't trying to get on fucking "Entertainment Tonight," or—she didn't care! She didn't care that she was on stage, with all these people watching, she didn't care what anybody might think—I mean like that fucking matters anyway, but we all walk around most of the time acting like it does matter. We're so fucking scared all the time, but she just—she just felt like it. And so she did it. I mean think about that for a minute.

It's powerful, right?

Analysis: *Apocalypse Apartments*

Type: Comedic
Synopsis

Apocalypse Apartments is a short play inside an evening of works commissioned by the Humana Festival's 2011 anthology exploring the end of the world.

Mick, Tyler, and Zoe are in Apartment 1A. Mick opens the play asking the other two to imagine Patti Smith, Robert Mapplethorpe, and Sam Shepard having a threesome.

Meanwhile, there is an apocalypse raging outside, and the three of them are in the apartment on lockdown. Zoe and Tyler are a couple. Tyler doesn't want to hear anything about this. He doesn't want anyone introducing the possibility of a threesome into his relationship, and he certainly doesn't want Zoe engaging, questioning, or encouraging Mick. Unfortunately, Zoe was listening to Patti Smith's song "Gloria" when the first wave of the apocalypse started.

Tyler is freaking out. He keeps re-sealing the windows and checking to see how much water from their supply has evaporated from the bathtub. Half the people they know are dead. They're not even sure if the Pacific Northwest exists anymore.

Zoe tries to comfort Tyler after his breakdown, but he rejects her. She sticks her hand down her pants and proceeds to masturbate. Mick follows suit. There is nothing particularly sexual between the two of them, but it kills the time. Tyler, furious, storms out.

Character Description
Mick, mid- to late teens

He thinks a lot about sex. He is completely oblivious to Zoe and Tyler fighting while he tells his story. He finds the idea of a threesome powerful and exciting. He finds nothing wrong in engaging in mutual masturbation with Zoe even when there's nothing sexual between the two of them.

Given Circumstances

Who are they? Three friends locked in an apartment together.
Where are they? Apartment 1A in a large unnamed city.
When does this take place? The present.
Why are they there? There's an apocalypse happening outside.
What is the pre-beat? This piece opens the play.

Questions

1. Can you state your objective in a simple, specific, and active way?
2. Whom are you talking to? Be specific and have a clear image.
3. Can you think of three adjectives to describe your character?
4. Whose apartment is this?
5. What does it look like?
6. How long have you, Zoe, and Tyler known each other?
7. Have you ever had feelings for Zoe?
8. Are you proposing a threesome among you all?
9. Does Zoe look like Patti Smith?
10. Are they a good couple together?
11. What is it about this story that turns you on most?
12. How big of a Patti Smith fan are you?
13. What do you want to do for a living?
14. What kind of apocalypse is happening outside?
15. What's would the couple's ideal response to this story be?

girl.
Megan Mostyn-Brown

ISAAC

Noticed her
like right away
first day of ninth grade.
She fuckin' skateboards to school
and she's good.
Like
not many girls who can pull that shit off
and be like for real.
And she's not one of those girls who travels in a pack.
You know how they do that?
And like individually you can remember their names and certain
like personality traits
but when they're together in the hallway
wearing the same fuckin' tank tops and jeans
and their hair's all long n' straight
n' like brushed a million times
you can't tell one from the other.
Seriously.
But you know I always notice Lucy.
It's just her n' her camera n' her skateboard.
And she don't have a lot of friends.
That takes balls
specially here
where you can see in the kids around you

who's gonna end up bein'
the million dollar whatever who lives in White Eagle
or the bitchy First Chicago bank teller
or the prostitute who hangs out in the park near the "Jesus Saves"
sign.
S'like I saw this "Twilight Zone"
from the fuckin' fifties
that shit's creepy
anyway these people end up on this town where everything looks
the same
like nothing's changed for years
and they keep trying to get out of this fucked up town
but they can't
then in the end the camera pulls back and you realize that the
town is this little play land that these really gigantic kids are playing
with and the people stuck in the play land will never get out.
That's how Aurora is man.
S'like a there's a fuckin' sad force field around the place.
You're destined to wither here.
Not me man.

Analysis: *girl.*

Type: Dramatic
Synopsis

This monologue is from Part 2 of *girl* and it's titled "We Did What We
Could with What We Had."

Lucy lives in a very small Midwestern town. She's youthful and sassy,
but she's seen a lot. She stands outside alone at night with a large duffel
bag and an atlas. This short plays is told through alternating monologues
by Lucy, her mother, and Isaac.

Lucy's mother is in her early thirties. She's been a waitress and a bartender for years. Lucy has always stood out. Lucy's dad left right after she was born, and they've never met.

Lucy doesn't dress like a boy, but she has a penchant for oversized, baggy clothes and she wears boys' high-top sneakers.

Lucy and Isaac have been friends since the ninth grade. Isaac was immediately taken with the girl who skateboarded to school, camera around her neck, and who had few friends. He admires her bravery in being who she is. They're not really boyfriend and girlfriend, but they are very close.

Lucy has only ever kissed one boy. She was twelve years old, and he was the son of a friend of her mother. Other than that, she is a virgin. Isaac overhears her lying to a group of girls about the strangest place she's ever had sex. He pulls her aside and tells her she shouldn't disrespect herself like that. That's how they became friends.

Lucy is unhappy here. She wants to leave town, get away from everything and everyone, and go somewhere where she can be herself without anyone judging her. Isaac comes up with a plan to get out of town. He wants to leave even before graduation. He is sitting in his car thinking about whether or not to actually go through with the plan while Lucy waits for him.

Character Description
Isaac, 17 years old
Isaac is Lucy's best friend. He wears his baseball cap to one side, his pants low, and two T-shirts even in the summer when it's hot. The story about how he met and befriended Lucy is in the above synopsis. He thinks there's a "sad force field around this town and no one can get out." Isaac compares Lucy to an avocado, tough on the outside but soft in the middle with a strong core. He has a dad who is not very nice. Isaac's dad wants him to join the army. Instead Isaac comes up with a

plan to steal his dad's Firebird, leave town, and drive into the sun with Lucy until they hit the ocean.

   Isaac does love Lucy, but not in the way she wants him to love her.

Given Circumstances

Who are they? Isaac is talking to the audience.

Where are they? He is sitting in his car at a gas station.

When does this take place? The present, 1:00 a.m.

Why are they there? He is supposed to pick up Lucy and drive to California.

What is the pre-beat? This is the first thing he says.

Questions

   1. Can you state your objective in a simple, specific, and active way?
   2. Whom are you talking to? Be specific and have a clear image.
   3. Can you think of three adjectives to describe your character?
   4. What does Lucy look like?
   5. Where do you feel her in your body when you think about her?
   6. What do you like most about her?
   7. Do you have any other friends?
   8. How long have you needed to leave this town?
   9. Are you attracted to Lucy?
   10. What's your relationship with your father like ?
   11. Why can't you wait until graduation to leave?
   12. What's waiting for you in California?
   13. Are you scared to steal your father's car?
   14. Do you think you'll ever see Lucy again if you leave?
   15. Where's the urgency in this monologue?

The Connector
Tim Murray

LEVI

He wouldn't stop hassling me about traveling. He kept saying "why don't you just do it!? Pack your things and go!" Cuz I have shit to do!! We can't all test out of math requirements, take four credits a semester and then just go see the world! He liked that I gave him shit. Liked it enough to give me a hickey. (LEVI *probably raises the roof.*)

We had a good time together. He took me to the beach, the movies and one day I convinced him to play tennis with me and he got all pissy cuz I kicked his ass. We casually dated for about a week or two, but I was busy with theatre. Plus, sometimes he could be a bit pretentious. I felt like he kept trying to prove how smart he was.

So . . . I may or may not have told some guys at school that . . . he was a huge douche.

I went back to my daily routine of rehearsals and classes and he actually followed his traveling dream. He went abroad the next semester to Madrid and while he was there he overdosed and died.

What do you do when something like that happens? Can you feel sad about someone dying that you weren't particularly nice to? Is that allowed? If you are sad won't people be thinking that you don't have the right, cuz you went around saying he was a tool bag with a weak net game? But then again if you're not sad will everyone think you're heartless? I mean the guy did give me a hickey the size of New Hampshire; we at least had a physical connection.

He wasn't my best friend or my brother or my kid . . . but he was someone's best friend and someone's brother and someone's kid. How dare I cry for him when these people have lost someone so special to them and I hadn't even spoken to him in months? One day I was deleting documents on my computer and came across a paper called "Who doesn't like to travel?" It was his application for the study abroad program that he had asked me to proof read for him . . . I never did. I started to read it and just . . . wept. Uncontrollably. I cried because I felt so badly about the way I brushed him off, I cried because he was so young and there was so much I know he wanted to see and do and I cried because . . . I missed him. That happens quite often actually. Out of nowhere in the middle of a random day I'll think of him and start to cry. Maybe I don't have the right to feel this sad about someone I didn't know super well. But I do. I do feel sad.

Analysis: *The Connector*

Type: Seriocomic
Synopsis

"I really want to find a man who is masculine, fun, sexy, spontaneous, silly, driven, understands my needs and isn't that into me."

And, with this line, so begins Levi's journey of self-discovery and acceptance. He is at a very large private university—think University of Miami—studying theater while searching for friendship and love, any kind of connection.

Murray's play is almost absurdist in structure. Levi's underdeveloped sense of himself keeps him from seeing people as they really are. Instead he sees them as archetypes, and they are named as such: Fun, Change,

Strong, Perfection. They aren't people in his mind, but bodies and personalities.

The above line of dialogue is spoken to Fun after a failed hookup. Although they don't hit it off romantically, Levi and Fun become fast friends. When Levi finds himself crushing on Change, Fun convinces him that the only way to win his heart is to play games and act uninterested. Obviously this doesn't work, and things get complicated.

Levi meets Strong, his first real boyfriend, when they work together at a theme park. The relationship seems serious until Levi finds Strong making a pornographic video for his ex, forcing Levi to end the relationship.

Levi then crushes on Perfection (are you sensing a pattern yet?). But when he takes Fun to a party that Perfection will be at, Fun hooks up with Perfection, causing a real rift in their friendship. All of these events force Levi to find out what kind of person he wants to be and what kind of people he wants as friends.

Character Description
Levi, late teens

Levi is a smoother version of Charlie Brown. He's personable, funny, socially aware, and all the while a little dorky. He spends most of his time with Fun, talking about sex and mindless gossip. He chose this school because it's one of the biggest party schools in the nation and has a twenty-four hour Taco Bell. Levi doesn't really like it here, though, because "when the weather is gorgeous every day you find yourself wishing for some sort of change."

Levi considers himself "gay fat"—not chubby but not in-shape enough.

Given Circumstances
Who are they? Levi is speaking to the audience.
Where are they? A university campus.

When does this take place? The present.

Why are they there? Levi is an undergraduate.

What is the pre-beat? This monologue starts the scene.

Questions

1. Can you state your objective in a simple, specific, and active way?
2. Whom are you talking to? Be specific and have a clear image.
3. Can you think of three adjectives to describe your character?
4. When did you come out of the closet?
5. What is your ideal guy actually like?
6. How do you define "casual dating"?
7. What exactly about this guy was pretentious?
8. What did he look like?
9. How did he make you feel?
10. Do you think you were in love with him?
11. What was his name?
12. Did you know he had a drug problem?
13. Why do you think you feel so sad about it all of a sudden?
14. What would you say to this guy if you could see him again?
15. What's the urgency behind this monologue?

Madame Melville
Richard Nelson

CARL

I don't know what I like yet.

How could I? And yes, I would very much like to borrow some books. That's why, to tell the truth—I stayed behind tonight. To see if I could—

And the reason I hardly speak in school or here—or at the films—is because I don't have anything worth saying. It's true. If you could hear some of my thoughts. Some of the things I've almost said? I laugh at myself all the time. Better me than you.

I'll tell you something that's true. At the beginning of the term, when the class books were handed out? I lined them up in my room at home. And measured with my hands their thickness and told myself—Carl, in a few months you'll know at least this much. (*Shows the width with his fingers.*)

Analysis: *Madame Melville*

Type: Dramatic
Synopsis

The action takes place in 1966 in the Paris apartment of Madame Claudie Melville. It's a time when the world was about to explode. Madame Melville teaches literature at the American School.

After one of Madame Melville's movie nights, Carl finds himself alone in the apartment with Claudie. They've just gone to see the very

famous surfing movie *The Endless Summer*. Claudie teases Carl that
he didn't like it as much as the French films about sex. Carl, although
young and slightly unsure, stands his ground regarding his opinion on
the film. Claudie tells him he's smart but could still do better in her
class. She wants him to assert himself more. Claudie asks Carl if he
didn't, perhaps, stay in the bathroom while people were leaving so that
he would, in fact, be left alone here with her.

Claudie takes cigarettes from Carl. She lies on the couch with her
feet pressed up against him. They drink wine together. Suddenly the
lines of education begin to blur. Carl asks her questions about her life,
along with questions regarding art, music, and literature. He's hungry
for knowledge.

Circumstances necessitate Carl spending the night at Claudie's
apartment. Claudie calls his mother, who approves, under the (incorrect)
assumption that Madame Melville is married. They sleep together.

The next day Ruth comes over and spends time with the two. She
quickly catches on to what's happened between them but reserves
judgment. Claudie takes Carl to the Louvre and shows him her favorite,
and least favorite, paintings. His education continues.

The two return to the apartment later on Saturday. Ruth tells them
Carl's mother came by. The headmaster gave her the address. The
three spend the evening talking more about art and music until Carl's
father arrives and, with barely a scene, takes the boy home.

Carl's parents make plans to send him back to Ohio. On his last
night in Paris, he arranges for them to take him to dinner close to
Madame Melville's apartment. He uses the excuse of going to the
bathroom to run to her apartment. They sit on Claudie's sofa, and she
plays *The Magic Flute* for them. Claudie, on her way to a date, asks
Carl to wait until she leaves before he exits her apartment.

Character Description
Carl, 15 years old
Carl is an American who lives and studies in Paris, France. His speaking voice is honest, simple, and thoughtful. Carl's father, a businessman, had been here for work and, when the project expanded, sent for his wife and son. Carl has a brother, who attends Cornell. He isn't a very good student, and he hates Paris. The city makes him feel stupid. It's on one of Madame Melville's movie trips that he sees his first (moving) naked woman. There is no music in Carl's house unless his brother is home. He smokes. Carl would like to be a writer one day, a poet. His parents go to church, but he doesn't. He lives in the Sixteenth Arrondissement.

Given Circumstances
Who are they? Madame Melville is Carl's teacher.
Where are they? Madame Melville's apartment in Paris, France.
When does this take place? 1966.
Why are they there? Madame Melville has taken her students out for a night at the movies, followed by a discussion at her home.
What is the pre-beat? Madame Melville has just played a Stéphane Grappelli record and asked Carl if he likes it.

Questions
1. Can you state your objective in a simple, specific, and active way?
2. Whom are you talking to? Be specific and have a clear image.
3. Can you think of three adjectives to describe your character?
4. Have you had fantasies about Madame Melville?
5. What feature do you find most attractive about her?
6. What does her apartment make you feel?
7. How is her apartment different from the one you share with your parents?

8. Do these evenings make you nervous?

9. Why did you pick this evening to lag behind when your classmates left?

10. Have you ever kissed a girl before?

11. What did the Grappelli make you feel?

12. What is your favorite book at the moment?

13. What did the film tonight make you feel?

14. What does your father do for a living?

15. Do you like Paris better than America?

Edith Can Shoot Things and Hit Them
A. Rey Pamatmat

KENNY

I told Edith that Mom would be watching her recital, and, in a way, I guess she really was there. Because if the distance between A and B and me and you and everything and everything else is infinitely divisible, then really my mom's only as far from me as you are now. Infinity.

She left. She loved us very much. And if it were possible, she would have stayed with us forever. She never would have left any of us.

It's the first lie I ever told Edith. The biggest one.

She . . . left . . . My mom and dad met in med school. Got married. Had us. And then Mom. She felt like my dad was not with her or us. Like he was distant, which he is. If you want proof that space cannot be traversed he's it, and eventually she got tired of it. She cheated on him. With my fourth grade teacher.

And she moved away—Ed doesn't remember this. She was leaving him. She was going to get a place with Mr. Simons. Bill. And then when they were set up, she was going to come get us. But then, a month later, she got her diagnosis.

A brain tumor. And she knew it would be too confusing for Ed and me, both things at once. So she left Mr. Simons and came back to my dad. But only for us. And only to die. She left him. She came back. She left us all. And then he left Edith and me.

Analysis: *Edith Can Shoot Things and Hit Them*

Type: Dramatic
Synopsis

Edith and Kenny, her brother, live with their father on a remote piece of property far from town. There is a house, a barn, and an orchard. Edith has very few friends but a very vivid imagination. She sits in the eaves of the barn with a pellet gun and dreams of being a "big, grown-up girl."

Edith and Kenny have a rough relationship with their father. He's mostly absent, preferring to stay at his girlfriend's house. He forgets to put money in the bank that they need for food and gas. Kenny spends most of his free time at his friend Benji's house. The mother of one of Edith's friends will call from time to time to check in and make sure Edith is eating the right things. Edith, tired of being alone all the time, tells Kenny to make Benji come over to their house. This small event precipitates a lot of action: Benji kisses Kenny while Edith does homework in the other room; Kenny and Benji go into the barn and begin a sexual relationship since there are no adults around. Kenny finds the nerve to call his dad and demand money.

Kenny and Benji carry on their relationship as secretly as possible. Kenny doesn't want anyone to find out their dad isn't there, because then the state would split Edith and him apart. Benji's mom, however, finds out about the relationship and does not handle it well. Benji moves in with Edith and Kenny.

Edith hears a noise late one night and shoots the pellet gun out the window. She ends up hitting Chloe, her dad's girlfriend, who has to go to the hospital and have a pellet removed from her shoulder. As punishment, Edith's father sends her to a private Catholic reform school. She escapes, and Kenny once again threatens their father into letting Edith stay under Kenny's "custody."

Character Description

Kenny, 16 years old

Kenny is a fairly average sixteen-year-old Filipino-American boy. He has mastered the art of not standing out. He cares deeply for Edith. He protects her, does the food shopping for her, cooks for her, drives her where she needs to go—when their father remembers to put money in the bank. And when their dad doesn't, Kenny always figures out what to do.

He can solve a Rubik's cube using algorithms. Edith says he's like a robot and doesn't even need to think sometimes. He just knows what to do and does it. He likes to read comic books filled with graphic sex. Benji is his best friend. They are sophomores in high school. The kiss between them is Kenny's first sexual experience.

Sometimes the pressure of taking care of Edith and running the house gets to be too much and he just wants to leave. But he stays. He doesn't like adults.

Given Circumstances

Who are they? Benji is Kenny's best friend and boyfriend.

Where are they? The front seat of Kenny's car.

When does this take place? Over the course of a few months in the early 1990s.

Why are they there? They were just at Edith's recital.

What is the pre-beat? Kenny has put his hand in Benji's and started stroking it.

Questions

1. Can you state your objective in a simple, specific, and active way?
2. Whom are you talking to? Be specific and have a clear image.
3. Can you think of three adjectives to describe your character?
4. What do you find most attractive about Benji?

5. How long have the two of you been friends?

6. When did you realize you wanted more than friendship?

7. What's it like carrying the weight of the truth about your mom?

8. Why not tell Edith the truth?

9. How does it feel to be the father and the mother in the house?

10. Do you feel abandoned by both your parents?

11. What does Edith look like?

12. How does she make you feel?

13. What made this the right moment to tell Benji?

14. What do you want to do with your life?

15. Are you in love with Benji?

Edith Can Shoot Things and Hit Them
A. Rey Pamatmat

KENNY

When we were in the hospital the other day. Me and Dad. He kept getting up—to get coffee or to call Chloe or to just go somewhere else. But I just planted myself and waited. And I watched him. I saw him. And he looked . . . so small. I mean, he's still taller than me, but he's not that much taller. Not anymore. And he just kept getting up, like he wanted to go—like he needed to. And I felt so bad for him.

I mean, Edith and I are here every day. And things go wrong all the time. But all you have to do is take a little time, deal with a little stress, and then fix things. But it's like he made all these mistakes, and he just left them there. And they got bigger. And if he had taken care of them while they were still small, maybe he would have realized it wasn't so bad, making mistakes. But now they were so big.

And I just felt so bad for him. He didn't know it was possible to just go home, and that there would be people there, and it would be okay. You could just fix it. And then you could feel good about it again. Even the part that was a mistake.

But why am I still scared, Benji?

Analysis: *Edith Can Shoot Things and Hit Them*

Type: Dramatic
Synopsis

Edith and Kenny, her brother, live with their father on a remote piece of property far from town. There is a house, a barn, and an orchard. Edith has very few friends but a very vivid imagination. She sits in the eaves of the barn with a pellet gun and dreams of being a "big, grown-up girl."

Edith and Kenny have a rough relationship with their father. He's mostly absent, preferring to stay at his girlfriend's house. He forgets to put money in the bank that they need for food and gas. Kenny spends most of his free time at his friend Benji's house. The mother of one of Edith's friends will call from time to time to check in and make sure Edith is eating the right things. Edith, tired of being alone all the time, tells Kenny to make Benji come over to their house. This small event precipitates a lot of action: Benji kisses Kenny while Edith does homework in the other room; Kenny and Benji go into the barn and begin a sexual relationship since there are no adults around. Kenny finds the nerve to call his dad and demand money.

Kenny and Benji carry on their relationship as secretly as possible. Kenny doesn't want anyone to find out their dad isn't there, because then the state would split Edith and him apart. Benji's mom, however, finds out about the relationship and does not handle it well. Benji moves in with Edith and Kenny.

Edith hears a noise late one night and shoots the pellet gun out the window. She ends up hitting Chloe, her dad's girlfriend, who has to go to the hospital and have a pellet removed from her shoulder. As punishment, Edith's father sends her to a private Catholic reform school. She escapes, and Kenny once again threatens their father into letting Edith stay under Kenny's "custody."

Character Description
Kenny, 16 years old

Kenny is a fairly average sixteen-year-old Filipino-American boy. He has mastered the art of not standing out. He cares deeply for Edith. He protects her, does the food shopping for her, cooks for her, drives her where she needs to go—when their father remembers to put money in the bank. And when their dad doesn't, Kenny always figures out what to do.

He can solve a Rubik's cube using algorithms. Edith says he's like a robot and doesn't even need to think sometimes. He just knows what to do and does it. He likes to read comic books filled with graphic sex. Benji is his best friend. They are sophomores in high school. The kiss between them is Kenny's first sexual experience.

Sometimes the pressure of taking care of Edith and running the house gets to be too much and he just wants to leave. But he stays. He doesn't like adults.

Given Circumstances

Who are they? Benji is Kenny's best friend and boyfriend.

Where are they? The living room of Kenny's house.

When does this take place? Over the course of a few months in the early 1990s.

Why are they there? Benji has moved in with Kenny and Edith.

What is the pre-beat? Kenny sent Edith to get their dad from the car because it's dinnertime.

Questions

1. Can you state your objective in a simple, specific, and active way?
2. Whom are you talking to? Be specific and have a clear image.
3. Can you think of three adjectives to describe your character?
4. What are you most scared of right now?

5. Is it nice to have Benji around to talk with?
6. Are you in love with him?
7. What quality do you find most attractive about him?
8. What's your relationship with Edith like now?
9. What does she look like?
10. What's your relationship with your father like now?
11. What does he look like?
12. How has it been being Edith's mother, father, and brother?
13. How do you want your relationship with your father to progress?
14. What do you want to do with your life?
15. What would make you happy right at this moment?

Edith Can Shoot Things and Hit Them
A. Rey Pamatmat

BENJI

I made a mix tape. For you. Some songs that made me think of you.

I put it in my schoolbag. And I wrote a note to give you with it. To pass to you in Pre-calc tomorrow.

I'm doing my chores—washing dinner dishes. I go in my room when I'm done, and she's sitting there holding the tape and the note. Her face is all twisted. Disgusted. And then she yells for my dad and brother, and when they come in, she shoves the note at me and goes:

"Read it. Aloud. To your father."

And I read. And she shakes and cries. And my brother swears. And my dad just stands there. I get to the end and I hear this . . . this crack sound. And she snapped it in half. Your tape.

I snatched it from her. I don't know why. It's useless now. She tried to take the note, too, but I held onto it, because I had to give it to you.

Analysis: *Edith Can Shoot Things and Hit Them*

Type: Dramatic
Synopsis
Edith and Kenny, her brother, live with their father on a remote piece of property far from town. There is a house, a barn, and an orchard. Edith has very few friends but a very vivid imagination. She sits in

the eaves of the barn with a pellet gun and dreams of being a "big, grown-up girl."

Edith and Kenny have a rough relationship with their father. He's mostly absent, preferring to stay at his girlfriend's house. He forgets to put money in the bank that they need for food and gas. Kenny spends most of his free time at his friend Benji's house. The mother of one of Edith's friends will call from time to time to check in and make sure Edith is eating the right things. Edith, tired of being alone all the time, tells Kenny to make Benji come over to their house. This small event precipitates a lot of action: Benji kisses Kenny while Edith does homework in the other room; Kenny and Benji go into the barn and begin a sexual relationship since there are no adults around. Kenny finds the nerve to call his dad and demand money.

Kenny and Benji carry on their relationship as secretly as possible. Kenny doesn't want anyone to find out their dad isn't there, because then the state would split Edith and him apart. Benji's mom, however, finds out about the relationship and does not handle it well. Benji moves in with Edith and Kenny.

Edith hears a noise late one night and shoots the pellet gun out the window. She ends up hitting Chloe, her dad's girlfriend, who has to go to the hospital and have a pellet removed from her shoulder. As punishment, Edith's father sends her to a private Catholic reform school. She escapes, and Kenny once again threatens their father into letting Edith stay under Kenny's "custody."

Character Description
Benji, 16 years old
Benji has an overprotective mother who doesn't want him going over to Kenny's house because she knows that there's no parental supervision there. His mother often goes through his room, rifling through his

belongings, and his older brother will tell her if and when she misses something.

He is very thin, too thin, and usually hunched over from carrying a gigantic book bag. His hair is a bit too long. He looks like someone who will one day go to MIT to become a civil engineer or to RISD to become an architect. He and Kenny became friends because Kenny needed someone to keep him awake in class.

He brings a dictionary over to Kenny's because he likes that there are words, scientific definitions, for what the two of them do together sexually.

Given Circumstances

Who are they? Kenny is Benji's best friend and boyfriend. Edith is Kenny's sister.

Where are they? The living room of Kenny and Edith's house.

When does this take place? Over the course of a few months in the early 1990s.

Why are they there? Benji has just shown up at their door.

What is the pre-beat? Edith told Benji not to be scared.

Questions

1. Can you state your objective in a simple, specific, and active way?
2. Whom are you talking to? Be specific and have a clear image.
3. Can you think of three adjectives to describe your character?
4. How long have you and Kenny been friends? Lovers?
5. What's your point of view on Edith? Do you like her?
6. What has your home life been like up until now?
7. What do your mom and dad look like?
8. Do you love them?
9. What does your brother look like?
10. Are you afraid of him?

11. What songs are on the mix tape?
12. How did you choose them?
13. How long did it take to make?
14. How does Kenny make you feel?
15. Are you in love with him?

Edith Can Shoot Things and Hit Them
A. Rey Pamatmat

BENJI

You know the first thing Ed said to me?

She walked right up to me and went, "I can shoot things. I can hit stuff."

I could never shoot someone.

And, like, when you're planning what groceries to get so you can make dinner and lunch and all the food for the week? I can't do that. I couldn't take Ed to school and extracurriculars and still get straight A's in Pre-calc and Chem.

I couldn't do half the stuff you can do. My mom tells me what to wear, and when kids used to be, like, "Your mom dresses you. Loser!" I didn't know why that was an insult, because I didn't really know that other people could do stuff. The only food I can make is a bowl of cereal. I still have my learner's permit. My mom does everything for me. Did.

You're not a loser. You and Edith. You're all alone in that house and sometimes it's creepy and sometimes you're running out of money, but you can take care of yourselves. I would just be helpless or scared.

The only person I care about now is you. So don't look at anyone but me. Just be scared for a minute. Okay? Be scared. And then we'll figure out what to do. And I'll help. I can help. You won't have to do it by yourself.

Analysis: *Edith Can Shoot Things and Hit Them*

Type: Dramatic
Synopsis

Edith and Kenny, her brother, live with their father on a remote piece of property far from town. There is a house, a barn, and an orchard. Edith has very few friends but a very vivid imagination. She sits in the eaves of the barn with a pellet gun and dreams of being a "big, grown-up girl."

Edith and Kenny have a rough relationship with their father. He's mostly absent, preferring to stay at his girlfriend's house. He forgets to put money in the bank that they need for food and gas. Kenny spends most of his free time at his friend Benji's house. The mother of one of Edith's friends will call from time to time to check in and make sure Edith is eating the right things. Edith, tired of being alone all the time, tells Kenny to make Benji come over to their house. This small event precipitates a lot of action: Benji kisses Kenny while Edith does homework in the other room; Kenny and Benji go into the barn and begin a sexual relationship since there are no adults around. Kenny finds the nerve to call his dad and demand money.

Kenny and Benji carry on their relationship as secretly as possible. Kenny doesn't want anyone to find out their dad isn't there, because then the state would split Edith and him apart. Benji's mom, however, finds out about the relationship and does not handle it well. Benji moves in with Edith and Kenny.

Edith hears a noise late one night and shoots the pellet gun out the window. She ends up hitting Chloe, her dad's girlfriend, who has to go to the hospital and have a pellet removed from her shoulder. As punishment, Edith's father sends her to a private Catholic reform school. She escapes, and Kenny once again threatens their father into letting Edith stay under Kenny's "custody."

Character Description
Benji, 16 years old
Benji has an overprotective mother who doesn't want him going over to Kenny's house because she knows that there's no parental supervision there. His mother often goes through his room, rifling through his belongings, and his older brother will tell her if and when she misses something.

He is very thin, too thin, and usually hunched over from carrying a gigantic book bag. His hair is a bit too long. He looks like someone who will one day go to MIT to become a civil engineer or to RISD to become an architect. He and Kenny became friends because Kenny needed someone to keep him awake in class.

He brings a dictionary over to Kenny's because he likes that there are words, scientific definitions, for what the two of them do together sexually.

Given Circumstances
Who are they? Kenny is Benji's best friend and boyfriend.
Where are they? The local ice cream parlor.
When does this take place? Over the course of a few months in the early 1990s.
Why are they there? Edith shot her future stepmother, and they're waiting for a health update.
What is the pre-beat? Kenny just had a minor meltdown.

Questions
1. Can you state your objective in a simple, specific, and active way?
2. Whom are you talking to? Be specific and have a clear image.
3. Can you think of three adjectives to describe your character?
4. Are you in love with Kenny?
5. When did you know you wanted to be more than friends?

6. Is it difficult to see him this scared and vulnerable?

7. What makes you feel scared?

8. What's your point of view on Edith?

9. Do you like having her around?

10. Is it better living with these two than at home?

11. Do you miss your family at all?

12. How has life changed over the past few days?

13. How can you help Kenny and Edith?

14. What's your favorite ice cream flavor?

15. What's the urgency behind this monologue?

Lessons from an Abandoned Work
Mona Pirnot

NATE

I hate sitting in desks. I can't focus.

When I was a kid, I missed lessons, crucial lessons, like learning how to tell time and stuff. I couldn't retain any of it because it was taught to me in a stupid fuckin desk.

I would just daydream about . . . I don't know. Anything. Not being in a desk.

I remember I didn't learn my multiplication tables when I was supposed to and my mom was quizzing me. We were at some embarrassing public place like Chilis and she would be like "seven times seven" and I would take a really long drink of my soda while I counted in my head. She caught on. She was mad. It was weird actually. She was, like, irrationally mad.

At Chilis.

I think I cried.

Analysis: *Lessons from an Abandoned Work*

Type: Seriocomic
Synopsis
"There is no 'right time' to work through the bullshit in your life. Don't abandon your work midstream when things get hard."

Fiona is having trouble relating to the world. Most of her college teachers spout generic concepts without probing the real depths of the issues at hand. Her fellow, overprivileged students parrot their parents or the news headlines they read on the Internet. Fiona wants more.

She volunteers at an assisted living facility for the elderly where she has befriended Arnaud, a stylish ninety-year-old Frenchman. They read Beckett's *Waiting for Godot* out loud to each other, and Arnaud probes Fiona about her life and pushes her to realize her true self, because he never got to be the best, most honest version of himself. Fiona feels closer to Arnaud than almost anyone else in her life, and as a gift to him, she enrolls in a playwriting class to write a documentary-style piece that questions what people are afraid of in their lives. Nate is the only other student enrolled in the class.

Fiona's parents expect her to pursue a career in politics in Washington, D.C. When they find out that Fiona is thinking about adding a theater arts minor, they threaten to kick her out of the house and cut off her tuition payments. Fiona moves out and into the dorm room of her best/only friend, Khaya.

Khaya, the polar opposite of Fiona, is more adventurous, more sexually open, and more savvy. She comes up with the idea of Fiona writing papers for students in order to make tuition money. Arnaud finds out about this, and he and Fiona have a fight. She says things to him that she deeply regrets. She has sex with Nate. The school discovers her deceit and suspends her. Khaya discovers she's pregnant. Nate offers no comfort. Arnaud dies, but he and Fiona make peace.

Edie, Fiona's playwriting teacher, is the one person who manages to motivate Fiona into getting back into the world. Fiona manages to reinstate herself into the school, and she changes her major to playwriting.

Character Description
Nate, late teens
Attractive, confident, and unhurried. Nate is also a playwriting minor but he has no major drive in life. He isn't quite sure what he wants to do. He approaches Fiona after their second acting class and playfully asks her out. Fiona, defensive about never having been approached by a boy, calls him "abrasive." He admits that he spent most of the class watching Fiona.

Nate tells Fiona that she's a writer. He finally convinces Fiona to go for a walk with him and takes her to his favorite "star-gazing spot" and proceeds to kiss her.

When things get serious, however, Nate doesn't have the ability to commit to Fiona or her troubles.

Given Circumstances
Who are they? Edith and Nate are classmates at college.

Where are they? They're taking a walk on campus directly after playwriting class.

When does this take place? The present.

Why are they there? Nate wants to show Fiona his secret spot on campus.

What is the pre-beat? Fiona has relented and given him one hour of her time.

Questions
1. Can you state your objective in a simple, specific, and active way?
2. Whom are you talking to? Be specific and have a clear image.
3. Can you think of three adjectives to describe your character?
4. What does Fiona look like?
5. What exactly do you find attractive about her?
6. Do you think she's a good writer?

7. What about this story do you think will charm her?

8. Why do you want to show her your secret spot?

9. Your teacher was pretty tough on you in class. Are you concerned about that?

10. What do you want to do with your life?

11. What other classes are you taking?

12. Would you consider yourself a motivated guy?

13. Why did you choose this particular college?

14. What do you want from Fiona?

15. What's the urgency behind this monologue?

3:59AM: a drag race for two actors
Marco Ramirez

LAZ

It's like a hundred degrees outside
And the asshole downstairs is watching porn again with the volume
all the way up
Like he wants everybody in the building to know,
And every time I close my eyes I feel the walls closing in on me
in my room,
'Cause even though it's just *me* in there now,
(My sister moved out like two weeks ago
And we don't know where she is
And we don't talk about it),
Even though it's just *me* in there now,
I swear to god the place is getting smaller.

. . .

And my aunt is coloring her hair,
And my mom is smoking cigarettes in the kitchen,
Screaming some shit about how I'm just like my father
But I just *go.*

. . .

And I just start driving,
In my flip-flops and gym shorts and Field Day T-shirt from the
sixth grade that still fits 'cause I was a fat little shit.

. . .

And I don't remember putting my foot to the pedal
Or first gear

Or second gear
Or stop lights
But they're all mine
And I'm gone.

. . .

I fly.

. . .

And next thing I know I'm down half a tank of gas
And I look at the clock,
And bro,
It's two o'clock
In the fucking morning.

Analysis: *3:59AM*

Type: Dramatic
Synopsis and Character Description

Laz is nineteen years old. He drives a Honda Civic that he refers to as his "escape pod." He still has to warm the car up even though it's hot outside. He bought it off a guy named Ray-Ray who works at the Chicken Kitchen. The car smells like curry and it's a stick shift, but Laz doesn't care because when he drives it, it feels like flying.

The other storyline is about Hector, a twenty-something fast food employee, forced to work double shifts because his wife is three months pregnant. He's tired and he wants to go home. At 2:00 a.m. he phones his wife to check in and finds out that she's at the hospital and she's lost their baby. Hector gets in his car and drives. He can't face his wife or the loss, so he just drives.

Laz is trying hard not to think about his sister. He sleeps in the same room but without her now. He has prayed that she's all right. He refers to himself as a "loser of all losers." His mother said he's not allowed to call her. If Laz tries to call her, the family will consider him a traitor and an embarrassment.

Laz can't find anything to play on the radio, so he just puts on static and sets the dial so that it plays loudly. Both men drive until it's almost 4:00 a.m. They put their cars in park and notice each other. Hector makes eyes at Laz like they're friends. And Laz revs the engine of his car. Without speaking, the two men prepare a drag race. They're on an old deserted road and they hit speeds upward of 120 miles an hour.

They describe the experience like being in the Millennium Falcon from *Star Wars* when it hits hyperspeed. Amazingly, they both survive the experience unharmed and energized.

The two men nod at each other and go their separate ways. Laz, feeling empowered, picks up the phone and calls his sister.

Given Circumstances
Who are they? Laz is talking to the audience.
Where are they? Laz's room or his car.
When does this take place? The present.
Why are they there? Laz couldn't sleep and needed to get out of the apartment.
What is the pre-beat? Laz just had the coolest drag race of his life.

Questions
1. Can you state your objective in a simple, specific, and active way?
2. Whom are you talking to? Be specific and have a clear image.
3. Can you think of three adjectives to describe your character?
4. Can you describe the Honda Civic?
5. You call the car your "escape pod." What are you escaping from?
6. Have you ever drag raced anyone before?
7. What was the most exciting part of the race?
8. What did Hector, the guy in the other car, look like?

9. The entire experience happened without you two exchanging a word. What was that like?
10. What's your home life like?
11. What do your parents do?
12. Do you have a girlfriend? A crush?
13. Do you have a job?
14. How do you pay for your car, gas, maintenance, et cetera?
15. What music do you listen to when you drive?

Four
Christopher Shinn

DEXTER

I love the fireworks. In the sky like that. That's unreal. That don't happen every day. Everybody standing there, all these people, under the bridge, on the water, standing there, or sitting on their blankets, looking up at the sky, everyone looking up at the sky like that, all quiet as it goes up and then cheering when it explodes and shit. Man, I love that.

That don't happen every day, you get all the people into the city like that, all of us who living out of the city go back in, and you got all the people, all looking up at the sky, and I know you say that there be, like, drunk people and kids running around being assholes, and niggers with guns and Latin Kings with knives and white boys with baseball bats and shit, but once the shit starts, you know, everybody stops. Everybody looks up at the sky. And is like . . . you know? Everybody's looking up there.

Anyway, you don't wanna go, that's cool, maybe we can see the sky get all bright from here, like the clouds lighting up or something, that's cool too . . . you just wanna be alone all the time, I had a grandmother like that, that's cool, only she didn't get that way 'til she got old.

Analysis: *Four*

Type: Dramatic

Synopsis

Four takes place in Hartford, Connecticut, on the Fourth of July in the year 1996. The action of the play centers around four very different people as they search for an intimate connection.

Abigayle is a 16-year-old African American girl home with nothing to do. Her father is away at a conference in Boston. Her mother is asleep in her bedroom. Her mother always seems to be sick. Abigayle always seems to be taking care of her rather than living the life of a teenager. Dexter, a young man she hardly knows, calls her out of the blue and asks her out. Initially she says no, fearful of leaving her mother home alone.

Meanwhile we meet June, a 16-year-old gay boy, who is waiting by a pay phone for a man to pick him up. That man happens to be Joe, Abigayle's father. He's not at a conference. He picked up June in an online chat room and arranged a meeting.

Shinn's play slyly takes on the American dream while exploring love, sexuality, and possibility. Joe says that going to the movies is "the most American thing you can do." June adds, "besides driving." Joe has the evening all planned out. He wants June to relax so that he's comfortable and ready for sex. Joe isn't a threat—he's not going to force June to have sex—but he desperately wants it to happen. So they go for a drive, they go to the movies, and they talk about books and politics.

Abigayle calls her dad to check in. Joe plays it off like he's in Boston. Then she calls Dexter and tells him to pick her up, but only for fifteen minutes and only because she's bored. The rest of the play jumps back and forth between "dates" as we see the couples try to get to know each other better. As in all of Shinn's plays, communication is an art form that not many people are capable of. Or they're not able to find the *right* person to speak their language.

Abigayle has Dexter take her to his house. Joe takes June to a motel. Both couples have sex. At the end of the play, all four go off in separate directions, feeling no more complete or connected than they did at the top of the play.

Character Description
Dexter, 19 years old
He's half Puerto Rican and half white. He spent the afternoon at a barbeque, calling Abigayle, persuading her to go out with him. He sells weed for a living, and Abigayle doesn't like it. His outfit of choice is baggy jeans, a T-shirt, and a baseball cap. He takes Abigayle for a ride. He tells Abigayle that she's acting bitchy (she is). He refers to his mom as a bitch. He is very attracted to Abigayle and wants to spend time with her. Dexter wants to take her to the park to see the fireworks, but Abigayle refuses. He knows that Mark Twain lived in Hartford. He plays basketball, and he's good at it. His grades are bad. Coach says he's the best Division II player he's ever had and wants him to transfer to a Division I school.

Given Circumstances
Who are they? Dexter and Abigayle are on their first date.
Where are they? Outside South Catholic High School.
When does this take place? The Fourth of July, 1996.
Why are they there? They're hanging out; Dexter is dribbling a basketball.
What is the pre-beat? Abigayle just said she's not scared of anything.

Questions
1. Can you state your objective in a simple, specific, and active way?
2. Whom are you talking to? Be specific and have a clear image.

3. Can you think of three adjectives to describe your character?

4. What does Abigayle look like?

5. What do you find most attractive about her?

6. Do you think she's out of your league?

7. You're a drug dealer. How did you get into that business?

8. Is it scary/dangerous?

9. Do you have a boss?

10. What is there to do on a date in Hartford, Connecticut?

11. Do you think you'll sleep with Abigayle tonight?

12. Does Fourth of July mean anything special to you?

13. Abigayle is being very quiet. What tactics are you using to get through to her?

14. Are you seeing anyone else right now?

15. What are you scared of?

Four
Christopher Shinn

DEXTER

I only like churches at night. When no one's in 'em. I stopped
going. To church. But I like 'em when no one is in 'em.

Like they seem more real or something. You know? When I
was a little kid I'd sneak into the chapel at South Catholic during
lunch. Before going and playing basketball at recess. I'd go into
the chapel and just sit there for a little while. I had problems,
you know. My mom and dad, they didn't get along. They was
always fighting. I smoked my first joint when I was seven. You
know that?

We used to go into this church. Me and my mom. After my
dad left. My mom decided we should go to Church. This was
the one she picked. She said 'cuz it was the ugliest church there
was and since she was ugly it was where she belonged.

I liked this church. I liked the basement. It was all quiet and
dark. I had sex in this church, lost my virginity. In the basement.
To this girl Ladrica. I was thirteen. She's dead now.

Analysis: *Four*

Type: Dramatic
Synopsis

Four takes place in Hartford, Connecticut, on the Fourth of July in the
year 1996. The action of the play centers around four very different
people as they search for an intimate connection.

Abigayle is a 16-year-old African American girl home with nothing to do. Her father is away at a conference in Boston. Her mother is asleep in her bedroom. Her mother always seems to be sick. Abigayle always seems to be taking care of her rather than living the life of a teenager. Dexter, a young man she hardly knows, calls her out of the blue and asks her out. Initially she says no, fearful of leaving her mother home alone.

Meanwhile we meet June, a 16-year-old gay boy, who is waiting by a pay phone for a man to pick him up. That man happens to be Joe, Abigayle's father. He's not at a conference. He picked up June in an online chat room and arranged a meeting.

Shinn's play slyly takes on the American dream while exploring love, sexuality, and possibility. Joe says that going to the movies is "the most American thing you can do." June adds, "besides driving." Joe has the evening all planned out. He wants June to relax so that he's comfortable and ready for sex. Joe isn't a threat—he's not going to force June to have sex—but he desperately wants it to happen. So they go for a drive, they go to the movies, and they talk about books and politics.

Abigayle calls her dad to check in. Joe plays it off like he's in Boston. Then she calls Dexter and tells him to pick her up, but only for fifteen minutes and only because she's bored. The rest of the play jumps back and forth between "dates" as we see the couples try to get to know each other better. As in all of Shinn's plays, communication is an art form that not many people are capable of. Or they're not able to find the *right* person to speak their language.

Abigayle has Dexter take her to his house. Joe takes June to a motel. Both couples have sex. At the end of the play, all four go off in separate directions, feeling no more complete or connected than they did at the top of the play.

Character Description
Dexter, 19 years old

He's half Puerto Rican and half white. He spent the afternoon at a barbeque, calling Abigayle, persuading her to go out with him. He sells weed for a living, and Abigayle doesn't like it. His outfit of choice is baggy jeans, a T-shirt, and a baseball cap. He takes Abigayle for a ride. He tells Abigayle that she's acting bitchy (she is). He refers to his mom as a bitch. He is very attracted to Abigayle and wants to spend time with her. Dexter wants to take her to the park to see the fireworks, but Abigayle refuses. He knows that Mark Twain lived in Hartford. He plays basketball, and he's good at it. His grades are bad. Coach says he's the best Division II player he's ever had and wants him to transfer to a Division I school.

Given Circumstances
Who are they? Dexter and Abigayle are on their first date.

Where are they? A small church Dexter used to attend with his family.

When does this take place? The Fourth of July, 1996.

Why are they there? They've been driving around Hartford all night.

What is the pre-beat? Dexter asked about Abigayle's father, and she said she doesn't want to talk about him.

Questions
1. Can you state your objective in a simple, specific, and active way?
2. Whom are you talking to? Be specific and have a clear image.
3. Can you think of three adjectives to describe your character?
4. What does Abigayle look like?
5. What do you find most attractive about her?
6. You two had sex tonight. Were you expecting that?
7. How was the encounter?
8. Abigayle continues to be quiet. How do you get through to her?

9. Why are you in this church?

10. You've opened up to her a lot tonight. What is it about Abigayle that makes you vulnerable?

11. Do you want to the night to keep going?

12. Do you want to see her again?

13. How does she make you feel?

14. Do you think you're good enough for her?

15. What's your relationship like with your parents?

The Curious Incident of the Dog in the Night-Time
Simon Stephens

CHRISTOPHER

I've decided I am going to try and find out who killed Wellington because a Good Day is a day for projects and planning things.

Wellington is a dog that used to belong to my neighbor Mrs. Shears who is our friend but he is dead now because someone killed him by putting a garden fork through him. And I found him and then a policeman thought I'd killed him but I hadn't and then he tried to touch me so I hit him and then I had to go to the police station.

And I am going to find out who really killed Wellington and make it a project. Even though Father told me not to.

I don't always do what I'm told.

Because when people tell you what to do it is usually confusing and does not make sense. For example people often say 'Be quiet' but they don't tell you how long to be quiet for.

Analysis: *The Curious Incident of the Dog in the Night-Time*

Type: Seriocomic
Synopsis

The play opens with Christopher standing over the dead body of Wellington, a dog belonging to his neighbor Mrs. Shears. Wellington has a large garden fork sticking out of his side.

The events of the play are being read aloud by Siobhan, Christopher's high school teacher. She serves as both narrator and character throughout the story. Christopher has an unstated medical condition that severely affects his ability to relate to people physically and emotionally. Although the condition is never stated, it bears a strong resemblance to Asperger's Syndrome, or high-functioning autism.

When the police come to investigate, an officer attempts to touch Christopher, who hits him. Christopher's father, Ed, comes to the station to retrieve Christopher and explain his condition to the police. They let him go. Christopher vows to find Wellington's murderer, even though Ed tells him to let it go. Christopher's investigation leads him down a path of discovery he never could have expected. He begins by going door-to-door in his neighborhood. Mrs. Shears won't speak to him. A kindly older woman, Mrs. Alexander, tries to befriend him.

Christopher believes his mother died two years ago. That's what his father told him. First Christopher finds out his mother was having an affair with Mr. Shears. Then he finds stacks of letters from her to him, some very recent, in Ed's room. She is alive and living in London with Mr. Shears.

He is detailing the events around his investigation in a notebook, which is what Siobhan is reading to us. Ed tells Christopher he threw his notebook away. While Christopher is searching for the notebook, he finds the letters and gets very upset and very sick. This is when Ed finds him. Their relationship is permanently altered.

Christopher swipes his father's debit card and leaves his small town of Swindon to find his mother in London—which he does.

Ed comes to London and finds him, forcing a sort of reunion among the family. Christopher chooses to stay with his mother but slowly begins to let Ed back into his life. Ultimately, Christopher passes his A level. Ed gets a puppy to give Christopher a reason to come over more.

Character Description
Christopher Boone, 15 years old
Christopher lives in a small English town with his father. He is fifteen years and three months and two days in the first scene. He suffers from a condition very similar to Asperger's syndrome; a high-functioning autistic. He needs precision and control in his life, a sense of order, in order to get through the day. Everything has a time and a place. He likes dogs. He is physically incapable of telling a lie. Christopher finds people confusing because they do a lot of talking without using any words. They also talk in metaphors. He needs his watch so he knows exactly what time it is. Christopher is a prodigy at math. He is preparing to take an A level (a very important test) and would be the first person in his school to do so. He has a pet rat named Toby. He would like to be an astronaut.

Given Circumstances
Who are they? Siobhan is Christopher's teacher.

Where are they? Christopher's school.

When does this take place? The present.

Why are they there? Wellington, his neighbor's dog, was just murdered.

What is the pre-beat? Siobhan has asked him how he is today.

Questions
1. Can you state your objective in a simple, specific, and active way?
2. Whom are you talking to? Be specific and have a clear image.
3. Can you think of three adjectives to describe your character?
4. What did Wellington look like?
5. Did you play with the dog a lot?
6. Have you ever seen a dead dog before?
7. Was it a violent and bloody crime scene?
8. What does Siobhan look like?

9. What do you like most about her?
10. What does your father look like?
11. If he told you not to investigate, why are you choosing to do so against his wishes?
12. Where will you begin your investigation?
13. Is this the first time you've disobeyed your father?
14. How many friends do you have, and who are they?
15. What's the urgency behind this monologue?

Exit Exam
Mara Wilson

MIGUEL

"Who is your hero and why?"

(*He snorts.*)

I find this prompt flawed because the word "hero" is completely subjective. To demonstrate, I'll assume that "hero" refers to someone who literally saved my life. Since I have never had a brush with death, the only person my life depended on would be the Spanish Padre who got my great great great et cetera grandmother pregnant on a Mission so many years ago. Without his unscrupulous breaking of the vows, I would not have been born.

However, the word "hero" in this sense has connotations that imply the person is to be respected, and God knows—pun intended—that I do not respect this particular character. "Role model" has similarly bothered me, because I feel that modeling my life upon another is contradictory to what I perceive as the meaning of life. Genetics, random chance, and perhaps cosmic forces have led to the creation of myself, and I am a completely unique human being.

However, due to time constraints and the simple fact that I *would* like to pass this test and graduate at some point, I feel compelled to stop arguing semantics and to acquiesce to writing about the topic at hand.

All right . . . if I interpret the word "hero" as someone whose achievements I admire, et cetera, then I suppose my "hero" is

Langston Hughes. I would not consider him a "role model" for aforementioned reasons, especially considering I am neither a poet nor African American nor a civil rights activist. I am, however, an artist, and I am inspired by him. Let me ask you something— and ignore the improper use of second person in what was supposed to be a formal essay, because I am talking to *you*, Mr. or Ms. Exit Exam Adjudicator: have you ever read Langston Hughes' poetry? It's fucking beautiful.

Yes, I said "fucking," you will survive.

His ability to not only create a living breathing model of 1920s Harlem, but to also touch and inspire someone like myself, so far away chronologically and otherwise, is truly heroic.

Analysis: *Exit Exam*

Type: Seriocomic
Synopsis and Character Description
This piece was written as a stand-alone monologue, so all of the factual information you need about the character and events can be found within.

Exit Exams are tests that many American students need to pass in order to graduate from high school. That would put Miguel anywhere between the ages of sixteen and nineteen. The first thing you'll notice about Miguel is how smart he is. He knows how to frame an argument, endow it with his point of view, and speak well.

The way he scoffs initially at the "Who is your hero question?" might make you wonder if Miguel has gotten this far in life on his own. He doesn't choose a parent or guardian as a hero. In fact, the only reference made to his family is the Spanish priest who impregnated an ancestor.

It's amusing that he spends three paragraphs avoiding having to answer the question. Is he stalling for time during those sections, or does he really want to argue the fact that he doesn't believe in heroes and role models? It seems that he has spent some time considering the question before answering, which leads me to believe that he really wants to argue and, more importantly, likes to argue in general. He has strong opinions and beliefs, and he is not shy about expressing them.

Miguel refers to himself as an artist but doesn't go into detail about what his art is. He only tells us he is not a poet. An African American poet who wrote about Harlem, the Jazz Age, and the Harlem Renaissance seems like a curious choice for an argumentative young Hispanic man. Miguel doesn't go into detail, but he does say that he finds Hughes's writing inspirational.

Be careful when approaching this monologue that Miguel doesn't come off as purely defensive. You must find the sense of humor, the devil in him that is knowingly using the exit exam to say something else about his beliefs. It will be easy to make Miguel seem like a know-it-all, but you have to endow him with a sense of passion and a true love of Hughes as a motivational and aspirational figure.

Given Circumstances

Who are they? Miguel is talking to the audience.

Where are they? He could be in his room or at school.

When does this take place? The present.

Why are they there? He has to answer this question and pass in order to graduate.

What is the pre-beat? Someone has asked him to speak/write on who his hero is.

Questions

1. Can you state your objective in a simple, specific, and active way?
2. Whom are you talking to? Be specific and have a clear image.
3. Can you think of three adjectives to describe your character?
4. "The audience" isn't specific enough for a partner. To whom are you speaking?
5. What do you want from them?
6. Do you really have no heroes, or is this a front?
7. Where did you first hear about Langston Hughes?
8. What's your favorite poem of his?
9. How does he inspire you?
10. Where else do you find inspiration in your life?
11. Do you like your high school?
12. Are you happy to graduate?
13. Do you have a lot of friends there?
14. What are your post—high school plans?
15. What do you think you want to do professionally?

Women's Monologues

Dig Dig Dig
Nikole Beckwith

CELLY

I guess I knew I couldn't bring Snowflake. But I figured if I brought her out here we'd at least get to spend a little more time together.

I took the long way. That's why I was late. I wanted to spend a little more time with my cat. We walked through The Sampson's Orchard. I guess it's the only orchard, so we could just call it Orchard. But if we did that here, we'd never call anything by name. There's only one of everything. School. Store. Diner. Doctor. Bus. We don't even have a Library, there's just a room in the Post Office with a bunch of books in it.

I took a class trip to a Library once. Five towns over, in Springfield. It took us half a day to get there. There was air conditioning and so many books they had ladders you could use to reach the highest shelves. It's not like I am obsessed with books, I mean, books are cool. But it was less about the thing and more about how many there were. How many choices. Or choice, period.

That's when I got to thinking about other places. Like, if there is a place with so many books, there must be other places, with so many other things. To choose from. Here, you just kind of have the things you have. And you're happy. End of story.

My parents both grew up here. They love each other. But would they? Like, would I love *War and Peace* as much as I do if I got to read *Catcher in the Rye?* I don't know. Not that I don't love loving *War and Peace*, I just want to know what else I might love. Or what might love me.

It's a little scary. When you think of it in reverse. When you think of being loved less in comparison. Or loved more by proxy. But you can't go your whole life like that, wondering if you love something because it's the only thing to love or vice versa. I guess my parents are lucky in that they never took a trip to the Springfield Library. Lucky that it wasn't built until after they were married. Like so many other things.

I guess with Snowflake, it's easy. I know she doesn't know how to compare.

Analysis: *Dig Dig Dig*

Type: Seriocomic
Synopsis

The play opens with Robin and Web digging a hole. They are about four feet, or waist deep, into it. It is a quiet night, and the only sounds to be heard are the crickets and the shovels. Robin and Web are teenagers. Robin is in charge. Once Celly gets there, two of them can dig at the same time while the other rests—that way they're in perpetual motion.

Web wants to make the hole wider so all three of them can fit into it, but Robin says it will look suspicious. We have yet to discover why this hole is being dug. Robin and Web are brother and sister. Web stops to eat a peanut butter and jelly sandwich on rye bread. For some mysterious reason, their mother only buys rye. Robin keeps digging. Celly is twenty minutes late.

Robin thinks they've dug down deep enough and that it's time to start digging forward. It slowly becomes apparent that they're tunneling out. If they're not down too deep, then they have a chance of escaping should the tunnel collapse.

Web reveals he left a goodbye note for their parents. He assumed that Robin did, as well. She assumed that he wouldn't. He left it in a Christmas bowl that no one really goes near. Robin warns him that he's to blame if they get caught. Celly finally arrives. Robin instructed them to bring five of their favorite things and two changes of clothes.

Robin has the entire route planned so that their digging doesn't bring them too close to anyone else's property. They don't have a particular destination—they just need to get out of this town. There's nothing to do.

At play's end they disappear into the hole and, Beckwith tells us, begin their journey successfully!

Character Description
Celly, early to mid-teens
Celly is twenty minutes late at the start of the play. Her real name is Cecilia, but Web called her Celly when he was five years old and it stuck. Web thinks the two of them should get married. She arrives with her backpack, a garden spade, and a cat carrier. Celly brings Snowflake, her cat, with her under the assumption that it's dark in the hole and cats are nocturnal. She comes wearing sandals but also has a pair of sneakers and workboots. Celly also left a note for her parents. There are three pairs of swimming goggles in her backpack. Once they are ready to tunnel, Celly opens the cat carrier and points it toward her home.

Given Circumstances
Who are they? Celly is with her two friends Web and Robin.

Where are they? In front of a hole in a small town where nothing happens.

When does this take place? The present.

Why are they there? They are digging their way out of town.

What is the pre-beat? Celly has stopped to change her shoes again.

Questions

1. Can you state your objective in a simple, specific, and active way?
2. Whom are you talking to? Be specific and have a clear image.
3. Can you think of three adjectives to describe your character?
4. What do Web and Robin look like?
5. Do you like one more than the other?
6. Who devised this plan to dig out of town?
7. Did you need to be convinced to do it?
8. Is there anything you love about this place?
9. Besides Snowflake and shoes, what else did you pack?
10. What's your favorite book?
11. Did you bring it with you?
12. What are you reading right now?
13. Do you love your parents?
14. Are you going to miss them?
15. What do you imagine life outside this town to be like?

Untitled Matriarch Play (Or Seven Sisters)
Nikole Beckwith

BECKA

This is stupid. Being young is stupid.

They say that "Youth is wasted on the young." But that is only true because youth is ruined by the old. Everyone acts like it's some big prize, but only because you are never really allowed to have it. When you are younger, growing up is all about your potential. And when you are older it's all about what you used to be. So when are you anything, really?

Maybe never.

But people act like it's some big privilege to be young. Something you're getting away with. And they treat you accordingly. Which basically makes being young feel like being a criminal. But not in a cool way. Just like in the way that nothing belongs to you. No matter how much is all around you, nothing is yours. Being young feels like being nothing. Which is what wastes it.

They should say "Youth is wasted for the young." And so here my youth is being ruined for me and then I'll grow up into something, likely less promising than my expired potential, and then I'll be like married to the idea of what I was and that will make me so fucking sad that the next young person will come along and I'll quietly wreck the best years of their life and the cycle continues.

I guess the next young person will be this stupid baby. When he's 15 I'll be 30. But it's different for boys, they are allowed to be young forever. Girls have to grow up for them. So maybe I will just resent him for other reasons. Or maybe I won't. Maybe I'll love him. But maybe the people you love the most are the people you resent the most. Because like who cares about the people you don't love? What do they have to do with anything?

Either way, I'm not having a good time.

Analysis: *Untitled Matriarch Play (Or Seven Sisters)*

Type: Seriocomic
Synopsis

The play's action revolves around a large family of women: Lorraine, her daughters, and her mother. It is the night before Lorraine's fifty-fifth birthday. Lorraine has bought flowers for herself to celebrate. Lorraine has asked them all here. They think it's for dinner, but Lorraine hasn't cooked anything. Karen tries to order a pizza, but Lorraine hangs up the phone, telling Karen she'll be single forever if she keeps eating like a single person. The discussion opens up to the fact that all of Lorraine's daughters are single. In Lorraine's mind if you're not married, you're single.

Finally the daughters pressure Lorraine into telling them why they're all here if not to celebrate her birthday. Lorraine announces she's having a baby, through a surrogate. When the girls tell Lorraine that she doesn't even like the children she has, her response is simply, "all the more reason to have another." This is a highly dysfunctional family. Not only do they suffer from communication issues, but none of them seem to like each other very much. Perhaps they love one another, but respect is a different story.

Lorraine wants a son. She believes daughters grow up to resent their mothers, whereas sons grow up to revere them.

The bickering continues. Each woman fights to be seen and/or accepted. Suddenly the surrogate, Sera, shows up. Sera is seven months pregnant. They attempt to talk about politics, but it's futile. The women are most comfortable when arguing, picking on one another, or telling the other what to do.

Beckwith's play slyly sometimes, aggressively others, skewers female dynamics, motherhood, sisterhood, aging, male/female relationships, and what it means to be a woman in America in the modern age.

In the midst of throwing the baby shower, Claire announces that she and the surrogate are petitioning to legally adopt the baby, and Becka puts up a fight. She wants a real sibling because her sisters are so much older than her. Unfortunately, and possibly because of her addiction to diet pills, Lorraine dies during the birth of the child. The surrogate actually has a boy. Becka says she will take care of him, if someone will take care of her. The remaining women in the family realize that they have to take care of one another.

Character Description
Becka, 15 years old
Becka texts when she is not talking and often when she is. She has three older sisters. She still lives at home with her mother. She doesn't want to hang out with her family and asks if she can eat in her room. When Lorraine says she has an announcement to make, Becka asks if she's dying. Lorraine oftentimes refers to her *three* daughters, forgetting she has four. Lorraine has the ability to forget her youngest daughter completely. Becka tells her mom she's a million years old. She's practical and knows where things are around the house. Becka tries to get a ride to the mall. No one takes her. She asks to go to her friend Caroline's house and takes one of the two birthday cakes. She comes home from Caroline's almost immediately and in a fury because Caroline bought

the same backpack as her. Becka needs a parent. She needs someone
to see and take care of her. She doesn't need another sibling.

Given Circumstances

Who are they? Becka is talking to the audience.

Where are they? The living room of Becka's house.

When does this take place? The present.

Why are they there? It's Lorraine's birthday, and she has announced
she's having another baby.

What is the pre-beat? Her three sisters have just yelled that the conversation they were having didn't apply to her.

Questions

1. Can you state your objective in a simple, specific, and active way?
2. Whom are you talking to? Be specific and have a clear image.
   "The audience" isn't specific enough.
3. Can you think of three adjectives to describe your character?
4. Have you ever thought about having a baby?
5. What is it like being the youngest child?
6. What's it like growing up in a family of women?
7. Did you know your father?
8. What does he mean to you?
9. What do your three sisters look like?
10. What does your mom look like?
11. Do you think she's too old to have a baby?
12. Does your family fight a lot?
13. Do you feel ignored all the time?
14. What do you do to make yourself seen?
15. Whom do you talk to outside of the house?

Great Falls
Lee Blessing

BITCH

I'm pregnant.

The father? I don't know.

I was a virgin 'til a little while ago. I mean, I had a boyfriend. We messed around and everything like everybody else. We did a lot of stuff, mostly just to get him off—

Anyhow, as virgins go, I was getting more "technical" all the time. Don't know why I was keeping it. Wasn't waiting to be in love or anything. But, given my special history, I guess I didn't . . . feel comfortable yet.

My boyfriend was totally frustrated. He wouldn't admit it, though. He was being sensitive, you know? I was getting pretty good at oral, but—it was obvious I was going to lose him if I didn't put out pretty soon, so—

I didn't know how it was going to be the first time. Since I was so "special." Since Dad had made me so special. I was afraid I'd get all insane and panicky with my boyfriend. So I asked a friend of his instead.

Kid we both knew, sort of. In our class, anyway. I told him I wanted to lose it: one-time, no biggie. I don't know why I picked him; I didn't like him. Maybe that's why. Anyhow, he said come on over, his folks were out of town. We could drink, smoke, loosen me up a little. Zip-zap, shouldn't take long.

And he was right. It didn't. Blood on the towel-he *did* put down a towel. Blood all over my legs. I was so drunk and stoned, I barely remember it.

Analysis: *Great Falls*

Type: Dramatic
Synopsis

Monkey Man and Bitch are in a car in The Great Northwest just driving around. Bitch accuses him of kidnapping her—a twenty-mile ride has turned into two hundred. Monkey Man made Bitch promise not to call her Mom, but a day into the trip she finally breaks down and does it. From there, the relationship between the two characters begins to get clearer.

Monkey Man is Bitch's former stepfather. He was married to her mom. Bitch has given them both these names because he acts like a monkey and thinks she's a bitch. They're not allowed to use each other's real names.

Bitch's mom goes off on Monkey Man but doesn't demand he bring her home. She makes them stop at a drug store so that Bitch can get everything she needs. He hangs up, and Bitch screams at him that he's not her father. He says they'll get a motel room. He really needs to talk to her. Bitch says no to a motel and demands they sleep in the car. After an uncomfortable night in the car, the trip continues and Bitch relents to a motel for the next evening. They're in the land of hot springs. He suggests they stay for a day and see the sights. He buys her cigarettes but books a non-smoking room. Bitch showers and sleeps almost in the nude. Monkey Man tries to talk to her, but she falls asleep.

He's taking her to all the sights his parents took him when he was a kid. He's trying to be a father to Bitch. She finally refuses to go any farther unless she can drive. Monkey Man relents. He finally confesses that had so many affairs because he was scared Bitch's mom would be the last woman he ever had sex with and he wasn't emotionally ready for the commitment of marriage. He feels terrible about it and wishes that Bitch and her fourteen-year-old brother would talk to him again.

Bitch tells him the story of how she lost her virginity to two men, how they forced her, and now she finds herself pregnant. There's a Planned Parenthood in Great Falls, and she wants Monkey Man to go with her to get an abortion and pay for it. He owes her for what he's done to the family. He does. The recovery takes longer than usual because the doctor finds that she also caught chlamydia from one of the boys.

They end their journey back where they started. Monkey Man gifts Bitch his car. She says she wrote him a haiku right before her procedure and asks if he wants to hear it. He tells her to save it, as this isn't goodbye.

Character Description
Bitch, 17 years old
She's a week away from turning eighteen. She's filled with rage and smokes. She tells Monkey Man that when he's in prison for kidnapping her, the other inmates will rape him with foreign objects, like spoons. She has probably lost her job because of this trip. At the drug store she buys a stuffed rabbit with tiny antlers (a jackalope). She names it Vicious Penis Destroyer. She accuses Monkey Man of reading her diary. He denies it. Says Mom left him because he's cheap. She also accuses him of having sexual fantasies about her. She would rather watch TV than talk to Monkey Man. She doesn't know whom she hates more: Monkey Man or her father. Bitch is always writing. She used to share her writing with Monkey Man and he thought it was beautiful. Currently she's writing haikus. She was abused by her birth father.

Given Circumstances

Who are they? Bitch is driving with her mother's ex-husband.

Where are they? In the car somewhere outside of Kalispell.

When does this take place? The present.

Why are they there? Monkey Man wanted time to bond with Bitch.

What is the pre-beat? Monkey Man has finally let Bitch take the wheel.

Questions

1. Can you state your objective in a simple, specific, and active way?
2. Whom are you talking to? Be specific and have a clear image.
3. Can you think of three adjectives to describe your character?
4. When was the last time you saw Monkey Man?
5. How has he changed?
6. Is he dangerous, or harmless?
7. Were you close to him when he was with your mother?
8. What have you learned about him on this trip?
9. You've been driving for a few days now. How does it feel to be away from home?
10. Have you written any poems since you've been gone?
11. How long ago did this rape occur?
12. Did you tell anyone about it?
13. Why does now seem the right time to talk?
14. Do you think you are a bitch, or come across that way?
15. What about him, physically and/or emotionally, reminds you of a monkey?

Sondra
Laura Cahill

JENNIFER

And you wanna know what Tonya Harris said to me last night? She said she had an abortion, and I should calm down cause it's really no big deal. Like she could possibly know more about it than me. And she said that in front of everyone.

I couldn't fucking believe it, so I was like, "Alright, I didn't want to say this but . . . " I just had to let her know she's not some big deal. Especially since everyone was listening. So I go "Yeah, Tonya? I think I know a little more about it since I had three abortions already." Alright? Okay? I did.

And so I go "I had two when I was with Pete when I was fifteen and fifteen and a half and one just two weeks before I turned eighteen." And that was from that guy Hurley I met at my last job. So that shut her up cause now she knows she's not Saint Theresa of abortions going around helping people with their feelings.

She has no idea what it's like, no fucking idea. Nobody fucking understands.

Analysis: *Sondra*

Type: Seriocomic
Synopsis

The action of the play takes place in working-class New Jersey. It's a town dense in population, intersected by highways, and just out of reach of anything special. It's the kind of place that would make anyone feel stuck.

Sondra is nineteen years old. She lives with Barb, her mother, in an old house at the end of a lonely street. Sondra works at the mall. She's the assistant manager of accessories at JCPenney, but she has plans to get out—out of this house and out of this town. Barb isn't going anywhere. She's a cocktail waitress, most likely born and raised in this town. She's divorced and on a manhunt. Barb has taken in a boarder for the spare bedroom, a working man named Joe. Joe works at Auto Parts Express on Route 9. He's also an assistant manager. Joe takes an instant liking to Sondra, not Barb.

Barb is constantly trying to make money. Joe is a way to get more money in the house. She also has a side business in which she sells watches designed to "align your electric currents preventing negative takeover." In essence, scam watches that are supposed to prevent cancer. Joe asks Sondra out, leaves her notes, and becomes an uncomfortable and dangerous presence in the house for Sondra. Barb is unaware of this and won't listen to Sondra when Sondra asks for help.

Jennifer is Sondra's on-again/off-again best friend. Most of her peers find Sondra strange. She writes in her journal all the time. She's not man-crazy. She has dreams of getting out. Most people in this town dream of getting through the week so they can party all weekend. Jennifer is pregnant again and about to get an abortion. Sondra is stable, so Jennifer has gravitated toward her.

Joe keeps making advances on Sondra that she keeps dodging or rejecting. Joe begins to sell watches for Barb and invites Bucky over to make a sale. They end up just hanging out and drinking with the girls. Jennifer takes an immediate interest in Bucky, because he's a man. They play a game called "truth or lie," and Sondra gets very drunk. Jennifer goes for a ride with Bucky, leaving Joe and Sondra alone. Joe confronts Sondra about being stuck up. In the final scene, Barb returns home from work to find Joe packing and leaving and Sondra gone. Jennifer returns without Bucky and sits on the stoop with Barb as they wait for Sondra. They're not aware of Joe's anger or intense feelings for Sondra.

Character Description
Jennifer, late teens

Jennifer is Sondra's best friend from high school. Her mother has recently kicked her out of the house but will, of course, let her back in eventually because she doesn't want to be alone. Jennifer is tough on the outside but still vulnerable and looking for love inside. She thinks Barb is a cool mom and wants Barb to take her to her abortion appointment, but Sondra says no. Jennifer asks Sondra to go with her instead.

Given Circumstances

Who are they? Jennifer and Sondra are best friends.
Where are they? The back yard of Sondra's house.
When does this take place? The present.
Why are they there? They're hanging out.
What is the pre-beat? This monologue starts the scene.

Questions

1. What does Sondra look like?
2. How long have you two been friends?
3. What do you like about Sondra?
4. Why didn't you two talk for a while?
5. Do you tell her everything?
6. How many boyfriends have you had?
7. Were the abortions scary?
8. Who took you to the clinic the previous times?

9. Do you and your mother fight a lot?
10. How much about your personal life do you tell your mother?
11. You tell Sondra you'd like a mother to take you to the abortion clinic this time. Why?
12. Who's the father of this child?
13. What do you for a living?
14. What do you want to do?
15. How do you want other people to see you?

Perched
Lila Feinberg

ZIP

I went to his funeral. By myself. And nobody at his funeral knows who I am in the first place—nobody even knows my name. I'm just . . . this strange, nameless girl, hysterically crying. And the best part was, I got *stung*. Right in the middle of it. And I've never been stung before in my life!

So, his brother, who looks exactly like him, takes the stinger out for me. And he tells me that I was stung by a worker-bee—and that they sting one time in their entire life. Because when they do, it draws out part of their insides, and they die. So they only sting when they are in grave danger. They are like these little disposable soldiers for their colony . . .

And then I start to think that this bee, the one that stung me, is Matan. I'm not kidding. I become so convinced of this—that he had, somehow, given me his venom, his insides, as like, the final goodbye he never gave me—I mean, I'm *obsessing* over it so much that I break out into hives! Just covering my arm! And his mother feels so badly—even though she is the one that just buried her son—that she loads me up with all these jars of honey from her farm, to take back home with me. And how could I say no? Even though I felt so . . . stupid, you know?

When I finally get to the airport, I'm stopped by security because I had packed the 20 jars of freakin honey in my carry-on bag. Of course they let me keep my tweezers which could gauge someone's eye out . . . But I had to throw out all of the jars, one by one, into the garbage—like I was conducting some kind of sacrificial cult ceremony in my bare feet, right in the middle of the airport. Like, goodbye wildflower honey! Goodbye citrus honey . . . Goodbye . . .

And the funny thing is—I realized that I had never actually *tasted* the honey. After all that. But even now, back home . . . I don't know . . . It's like I can't rid myself of its stickiness. I am sticking to things. Or things are sticking to me. I can't really tell which.

Analysis: *Perched*

Type: Seriocomic
Synopsis

The play takes place in New York City and Israel. It opens with Zip waking up naked in bed next to Jed, an indie/hipster rocker. Zip doesn't remember anything about the night before. She suddenly remembers why she wasn't supposed to go home with Jed—she has a paper due at 9:00 a.m. Jed has a girlfriend, and they're in love but they have an open relationship. Jed asks her to sing in his band. Zip can't do it, though, because she's taking a trip to Israel. Jed sees that Zip has gotten her period in the bed and makes so she takes the sheets to get dry cleaned.

Zip and Becca go on their birthright trip to Israel. They have been friends since they were kids at summer camp. Love, sex, and relationships are the constant topic of conversation. Becca confesses to Zip that she and her hedge-fund boyfriend are secretly engaged and moving in together. That means that Zip and Becca are not going to look for an apartment together anymore.

On the bus a young soldier named Matan strikes up a conversation with the two girls. Although he seems interested in Becca, it's Zip's uniqueness that really begins to intrigue him. Matan thinks there is only one type of love, whereas Zip thinks there are a million. She and

Matan start to fall for each other. He asks her to delay her return to New York and come with him to his honey farm after the trip. Matan and Zip are suddenly pulled apart when he is called back to fight because the cease-fire in Gaza gets violated.

Zip and Becca are stuck in a Jerusalem hotel because Zip has hurt her ankle. While she's changing the bandage, Matan calls and talks to Becca. He says he's coming through town and needs to give something to Zip, and asks if they'll be at the hotel. Becca says yes, but then Zip gets the idea to go back to Tzfat and leaves. For some reason, Becca doesn't tell Zip about Matan. Matan shows up with a lotto ticket from an art gallery he visited in Tzfat with Zip. He asks Becca to give it to her at some point. Zip finds it, and she and Becca have a huge fight because of all the lies Becca has been telling. Becca admits to sleeping with a guy a few nights ago. Then the trip leader arrives and tells the girls that Matan is dead.

The action jumps forward and back to New York. Zip is preparing to sing with Jed's band. Becca shows up, and Zip tells her about the funeral. The girls make up.

Character Description
Zip, late teens
Zip's full name is Tziporah, meaning "little bird," but she never tells anyone that. Zip is a hot mess. She's lost but searching, an undergrad at Sarah Lawrence. When she wakes up in bed with Jed, she realizes she's been in this position before. She says she shouldn't drink, because, unlike most people, she lies when she drinks instead of telling the truth. The title of her paper is "The Furious Flowering of Feminist Poetry." It's her dream to sing. She just did a musical version of *Long Day's Journey into Night*. Zip is always there for Jed when he needs her (read: when he texts her for sex at 1:00 a.m.). Zip and her friend Becca take a birthright trip to Israel. She loves the show *Rent*. She thinks Becca

is compromising by getting married. Her parents have been married for a million years. She never knows what she wants, but she knows what she doesn't want.

Given Circumstances

Who are they? Zip and Becca used to be best friends.
Where are they? The bathroom of a Lower East Side music venue.
When does this take place? The present.
Why are they there? Zip is about to perform with a band.
What is the pre-beat? Becca has just given Zip a remembrance from Matan.

Questions

1. Can you state your objective in a simple, specific, and active way?
2. Whom are you talking to? Be specific and have a clear image.
3. Can you think of three adjectives to describe your character?
4. When was the last time you saw Becca?
5. What event precipitated your fight and separation?
6. How did your experience in Israel change you?
7. What was it like to go to Matan's funeral on your own?
8. Where do you feel Matan in your body when you think about him?
9. Did you love him?
10. How has that experience changed your relationship with men?
11. How has that experience changed your relationship with New York City?
12. How does it feel to have this remembrance of Matan in your possession now?
13. Do you forgive Becca?
14. Are you excited or nervous to sing in front of people in a few minutes?
15. What's the urgency behind this monologue?

Burnt Orange
Lila Feinberg

AVERY

Maybe this is what we needed. Stars like spilled salt . . . The yellow smudges of window light. A crescent moon. The trumpeting of cab horns in the distance . . . I love roofs.

Now you've said it. Now it's out in the air. In this night. It's dispersed. Like a million molecules . . .

(*She remembers her mother's ring on her finger.*)

Look, I found her ring . . .

I remember my mom used to play piano for us, when we were young—it was like watching a racehorse in slow motion, the way her fingers would glide through space. Now she can't even wear her wedding band. Her hands are shriveled up into these little clenched balls. Watching my dad try to open them up and stretch them out . . . . She can't even pick up a fork anymore. He has to cut up her food into these miniscule pieces as if she were a baby. She tries to picks them up with her fists . . . I can't even watch.

Remember that one night when the entire city was enveloped in the smell of maple syrup? And they found out that it was just some factory in New Jersey that manufactured like, artificial food flavors? I don't know, I was just thinking about that . . .

How there is so much we can't possibly solve, and so many lost things that will never be found . . . all we're left with are these raw gaping spaces where they used to exist, you know? But that maple syrup . . . So it wasn't a mystery of the universe, after all. But still, it floated all the way here, to us, on this lonely island,

and it made the air so sweet and so full that night it didn't even matter . . .

Analysis: *Burnt Orange*

Type: Dramatic
Synopsis

The play takes place in a doorman building on the Upper East Side. Avery shows up with a mountain of baggage. She's not moving in, she's "migrating." Avery is coming to Jane's apartment but is greeted by Hunter, Jane's son. Apparently Jane has sublet his room without letting him know. Avery has already paid $1,000 for the month, so she has to stay; that was all the money she had.

While Avery gets the rest of her stuff, Hunter confronts his mother. She says they need the money and he promised he was going to return to school this year. Hunter asks why she didn't ask his father for money, and Jane explains that his new wife won't allow it now that they are expecting a baby. Avery finds some journals and newspaper clippings in a drawer that pique her interest.

Harrison, Avery's hedge-fund nonboyfriend, wants to spend more time with her, but he's picked up cues from her that say "back off." He's set up an oxygen-controlled tent in his bedroom. Avery has a panic attack in the tent during sex and leaves.

Avery has a dream about Nate, Jane's young son who's in the journals and the clippings. She wakes up when her bed collapses. Hunter helps her screw the bed together. He asks Avery if she ever gets sick of playing some role—something she thinks she should be. Avery answers, "No that's the thing—I think we only ever get sick of playing ourselves." Hunter tells Avery that the room she's staying in used to be his brother Nate's. Hunter found him dead at fifteen. Avery gathers her stuff and goes even though Hunter insists that she stay.

Avery's mom has a serious accident. After spending a week in the hospital with her mother, Avery returns to the apartment. The ghost of Nate begins appearing to Avery, not just in dreams but all the time. Avery breaks up with the hedge fund, makes peace with Hunter, and goes off into the world; maybe she goes home for once.

Character Description
Avery, late teens
Avery is allergic to dogs, and there's a pit bull in this apartment. She wears too-short cut-offs. She's spatially ignorant. She refers to herself as the "urban equivalent of Sisyphus," constantly moving all of her stuff around New York without the ability to rest. The other metaphor she uses to describe the moving is a "psychological game of Chutes and Ladders." She's been moving endlessly, housesitting and crashing wherever she can. She's periodically gluten-free. Avery says she found the apartment through a Craigslist ad. But actually her mother has advanced MS and is a client of Jane's, who practices healing arts. She's sleeping with a much older hedge fund manager named Harrison. Avery is an aspiring artist, and she works as an assistant in an art studio. She dates an older guy because there's nothing at stake, no emotional risk, and no potential future. Avery wants to be baggage-less and mysterious. She has taken something from every apartment she's stayed in.

Given Circumstances
Who are they? Hunter is the son of the woman Avery rents a room from.
Where are they? The roof of the apartment building in Manhattan.
When does this take place? The present.
Why are they there? Avery needed to get out of the apartment.
What is the pre-beat? Avery has just ended a long-term sexual relationship.

Questions

1. Can you state your objective in a simple, specific, and active way?
2. Whom are you talking to? Be specific and have a clear image.
3. Can you think of three adjectives to describe your character?
4. What is the air on the roof like?
5. Are you attracted to Hunter?
6. He's been pretty mean and standoffish to you this past month. What can he do for you now?
7. What's the view from up here like?
8. What did Harrison, the guy you just broke up with, look like?
9. Why did you sleep with him for so long?
10. Were you attracted to his age and power?
11. Your mom is very sick. Are you worried about her?
12. How often have you visited her in the hospital?
13. Why won't you live at home?
14. Has Jane provided any kind of maternal support for you over the past month?
15. Is this what you imagined your life to be?

Baby Girl
Edith Freni

ELISE

I'm not saying anything. We just need a place to stay tonight. I'm not saying shit to him about anything, all right, but Paddy's right, it isn't OK for me to have you sleeping in a car. And sitter won't barter with me anymore. Bottom line: we can't do it just the two of us. I need you to know that NOTHING is set in stone. I have a lot of thinking to do. Your daddy and I need to sit down and hash things out.

He isn't so bad, right? I mean he isn't so good either but he is your father and maybe he does get to have a say in things? I did love him at some point, right? Maybe . . . Yes. I did. And he damned well loved me. He might even still. Men are fucking ridiculous. Learn that lesson now. They don't know what they want or how they feel so it's our responsibility to tell them. So maybe if I just tell him . . .

It's important for me to know that you know that you came from someplace nice.

You're such a good baby. You never complain about anything. How do you do that? You're gonna be a good kid too. And I'm gonna do the responsible thing for you, whatever that means. I am gonna make sure that whoever raises you, does it right. No matter what, no matter what happens, I am going to love you. No matter where we end up, I'll always be your mommy. That's the one thing I know for sure right now.

OK.

Analysis: *Baby Girl*

Type: Dramatic
Synopsis

The play begins with Elise, our main character, in a restaurant kitchen asking Patrick for a job. She's recently been accused by her employer of stealing pills and, subsequently, fired. She desperately needs a job because she's a new mother. Patrick is her ex. He rebuffs her physical and emotional advances and sends her off with $100.

Richie is the father of Elise's baby and they came to a mutual decision that he wouldn't be a part of the baby's life but, of course, here he is. Elise hasn't named the baby girl yet, but she has given her Richie's last name, Higgins. Richie's solution to the financial problem is for Elise to sell the baby, and the two of them can split the money. Elise hates this idea and goes to Jason Higgins, her ex and Richie's brother. Jason will help Elise in exchange for sex or a date. Sensing no answer, Elise breaks down and finds herself at the motel where Richie stays, considering the option of selling Baby Girl.

Elise is a master of sexual and emotional manipulation, and she tries to seduce Richie again, but he calls her out on it, saying she coerced him into sleeping with her the first time, when he had no interest. Richie has other things on his mind—he's transitioning and having difficulties with the process.

A lawyer comes over and Elise asks many questions about what will happen to Baby Girl, where she'll end up, whom she'll end up with, et cetera. She figures out this lawyer, named Kush, is actually Richie's lover and they're planning on keeping Baby Girl for themselves. Elise gets locked up for stealing drugs, and Richie and Kush take Baby Girl. Patrick comes to the rescue, saying he'll help Elise find them.

Character Description
Elise, late teens
Elise is a new mother, unemployed, extremely sexual and aggressive but with no real sense of direction. She used to abuse drugs but has cleaned herself up because of Baby Girl. She can be physically and emotionally manipulative. She has no real home to go to anymore.

She and Baby Girl have been sleeping in her car for two weeks. She has no other choice. She can't go to her family, and her ex-boyfriends are providing little aid.

Elise has a self-destructive streak. Her relationship with Patrick ended when she brought a married couple home back to Patrick's place and had sex with them in his bed, but without him there.

She believes she'll be a different person if and when she gets out of New York.

She's known for her "brass balls." She's tough, no-nonsense.

Given Circumstances
Who are they? Elise is talking to Baby Girl.
Where are they? The Breezy Motel off the Long Island Expressway in Queens.
When does this take place? The present.
Why are they there? Elise is stuck there until she can make a plan.
What is the pre-beat? Elise's ex-boyfriend has just asked for sex in exchange for help.

Questions
1. Can you state your objective in a simple, specific, and active way?
2. Whom are you talking to? Be specific and have a clear image.
3. Can you think of three adjectives to describe your character?
4. Does Baby Girl look like you? Richie?
5. How active and responsive to you is she?

6. Do you love her?

7. Would you keep her if you could?

8. How come you carried the pregnancy all the way through?

9. Did you ever consider adoption or abortion?

10. What does Richie look like?

11. Does the baby look like him?

12. How does it feel to be staying in a motel room after sleeping in a car for so long?

13. How difficult is it to ask all of your ex-boyfriends for help?

14. Where are you parents in all of this?

15. What's the urgency behind this monologue?

Cutting
Kathleen Germann

FRANKIE

I was never even scared. Not even the first time. I remember it was a Friday afternoon, right after volleyball, and we had just made play-offs. It was the last day before break and all the girls were talking about where they were going for vacation and the trips they would be taking with their families and all the stuff they would get, like, all the iPads, and boots, and clothes and junk.

And I didn't feel it. I wasn't excited about break, or the game, or anything. Nothing. I was just thinking how I majorly messed up Ms. Klein's trig test. And the same thought just kept spinning over, and over, and over in my head. I had screwed up the last problem. And getting that problem wrong could mean that I don't make the top one percent or get into an Ivy; and how missing one random test could decide the rest of my life. And when I got home I went straight to my desk to see what I did wrong. That's when I saw the scissors.

When I picked them up I looked down at my own hand and I didn't recognize it. I knew that it was my hand, but I felt like it didn't belong to me. It was not part of me. It was like I was living outside of my own body for a minute. I don't know why I started doing it—I just wanted to know what it would feel like.

And for the first time I felt like everything was going to be ok. I felt alive. I was tingling and stinging and I didn't want to die, I just wanted to feel something.

And now I do it every day.

Analysis: *Cutting*

Type: Dramatic
Synopsis and Character Description

This piece was written as a stand-alone monologue, so all of the factual information you need about the character and events can be found within.

Frankie is a high school student, most likely between the ages of fourteen and sixteen. She's on the volleyball team and they've just made play-offs, which leads me to believe she's fit, sports-minded, and talented.

It also appears that she's suffering from severe depression. Her inability to get excited about her success is one major clue. Also, there's her inability to stop her mind from thinking the same thought over and over again, dwelling on one trigonometry test and how its results could negatively affect her entire future. Making the one percent and getting into an Ivy League school could be a pressure put on her by her parents, by herself, or both. Frankie is a perfectionist and driven to succeed.

Germann's description of the cutting is very specific and vivid, so your imagination of it must be the same. Obviously the cutting allows Frankie the ability to get outside of her body and her mind while simultaneously allowing her control over something in her life. When you're a teenager, it sometimes feels as if nothing is in your control. So even though the cutting may be painful, damaging, and permanently scarring, it's Frankie who gets to control it.

There must be more issues at play than the ones Germann spells out in this monologue, so it's important for you to create a long list of events and issues that lead Frankie to this place. Frankie's home life and school life must be vividly realized for you. The pressures of school—academics, sports, extracurricular activities—must also be very specific. The list of things that must be accomplished, and accomplished well, should seem never-ending. Then add to that the pressures of fitting in with your friends and attracting potential love interests. What are all the things that lead Frankie to cut?

Given Circumstances

Who are they? Frankie is talking to the audience or an unknown person.

Where are they? Frankie's room or a doctor's office or somewhere you choose.

When does this take place? The present.

Why are they there? Frankie is finally admitting to cutting.

What is the pre-beat? This speech stands alone, so it's up to you.

Questions

1. Can you state your objective in a simple, specific, and active way?
2. Whom are you talking to? Be specific and have a clear image.
3. Can you think of three adjectives to describe your character?
4. How long have you been cutting?
5. What about the person you're talking to sparked the confession?
6. Have you ever told anyone else about this?
7. How many cuts do you have?
8. How do you hide them?
9. How often do you cut?
10. Do you think about the cuts/cutting often?
11. How long have you played volleyball?
14. Do you find it a pressure, or an escape?
15. What other pressures do you have on you right now?
16. Do you want to stop cutting?

How We Got On
Idris Goodwin

LUANN

Sometimes when I'm bored at church I try to rhyme things in my head. Whatever is in the room. *Chair, people, hair, steeple, light, bench, white, inch.* Then challenge myself. Two-word rhymes. *Hymn-maker, thin-wafer.* I always loved rhymes. You know. Ever since I heard Melle Mel's "The Message."

My sisters used to love it. Have me do it when their friends were around. But they'd shush me whenever my mom or dad would come in. Especially my dad. He'd say, "I'm not trying to hear that. That's excuse music."

But I couldn't stop. Rhymes are made to stick in your mind. He'd say, "There is no training. I couldn't get in the NBA without training."

But I couldn't stop. Rhymes are made to stick in your mind. Rhymes have so much power, right? You can come up with something that takes over somebody's . . . brain! One time he heard me singing "The Message" and man, *woooo*, he just went upside my head. I stopped singing that song. But I couldn't stop rhyming. I came up with my own rhymes instead.

He'd find 'em and rip 'em up! So I just stopped writing. On paper. But now, I want them recorded. I want everybody to hear 'em to get my rhymes stuck. You know?

Analysis: *How We Got On*

Type: Dramatic
Synopsis
"Hip Hop is body/toasting is the spirit.

Hip Hop culture is 15 years old/Rap music—younger—but it's on the move."

The play takes place over the summer of 1988 in Middle America, in a town that feels like nowhere.

Hank and Julian go to different schools, but both fancy themselves the "fresh prince" of The Hill. "Fresh Prince" is a reference to rapper/actor Will Smith and his popular sitcom *The Fresh Prince of Bel Air*. Hank is hungry for success. He challenges Julian to a rap-off, because there can't be two rappers on The Hill. It turns out that the two boys went to the same basketball camp together several years ago, but once they were put on separate teams they never spoke again.

A character called "The Selector" appears throughout the play. She serves many purposes, and in this instance she explains the rules and techniques necessary to win the rap battle: metaphor, simile, hyperbole, and alliteration. The unspoken rule is that it's better to go second in the battle because people will remember you. This battle takes place in the mall parking lot.

Julian, who's not quite as serious about all of this as Hank, wins the battle and takes off on Hank's bike. Hank finds him at work a few days later. He asks for his bike back, and Julian asks Hank to write rhymes for him. Julian has a better performance personality, and Hank has more precision with words. The Battle of the Bands is coming up, and Julian wants to win. Hank agrees, but they end up losing. Hank's words are almost too smart.

The boys buy recording equipment and begin making and passing out cheap records. They also spend a lot of time fighting over songwriting. Hanks finally breaks and punches Julian, storming out. This break causes him to find real inspiration, and he finally writes a truly great rap.

Meanwhile, Luann finds their demo at a grocery store and finds the boys, asking if she can rap with them. She feels as stuck on The Hill as the two boys do.

Hank's father threatens to take away the recording equipment, until he finally hears a rap and begins to understand it as a kind of poetry.

Character Description
Luann, early teens
Her father is Nat Finnis, a center for the NBA. She doesn't like sports but is highly competitive. Her father doesn't like or support rap. Luann sees right through Julian's facade, realizing he memorizes all his raps ahead of time—he doesn't have the ability to make up a rap on the spot. She schools Hank: "there will be mistakes, find inspiration from your surroundings, and don't forget the joy."

Given Circumstances
Who are they? Luann and Hank are new friends.
Where are they? It's not specified in script. Hank's room, Luann's room, or a public place.
When does this take place? The summer of 1988.
Why are they there? Luann wants to partner with Hank and Julian.
What is the pre-beat? This is the beginning of the scene.

Questions
1. Can you state your objective in a simple, specific, and active way?
2. Whom are you talking to? Be specific and have a clear image.
3. Can you think of three adjectives to describe your character?

4. When did you discover rap?

5. When did you discover you had the ability to create raps?

6. How did you discover Hank and Julian?

7. What can you bring, artistically, to their partnership?

8. What's life in the suburbs like?

9. Do you wish you lived in the city?

10. How many raps have you written?

11. Whom do you show them to once they're finished?

12. Do your write every day?

13. Who are your friends at school?

14. Where do you find inspiration?

15. What's the urgency behind this monologue?

Strike-Slip
Naomi Iizuka

ANGIE

Why do you want to learn Korean? It's not like you're not going to remember. You're going to forget.

I like this place. You feel like you're on top of the world. It's like you can see the whole city down below and it's all like twinkling. Look at all those cars. They look so tiny from up here. Think about all those people just like in their own little worlds. Like they don't even think about what's out there. It's like they're trapped, you know. And they think that's all there is. It's like their worlds are so small and they never even wonder what else there is out there.

Rafi, I want to go away.

Fiji—It doesn't matter. It doesn't matter where. Just somewhere else, anywhere else. Let's just go, Rafi, just you and me.

Now, tonight. I want to go tonight.

Cause we talk about all these things. And you tell me this stuff, you tell me that you love me, you tell me that we're going to have this life, that we're gonna go and have this whole life together, but you don't mean it. You don't mean any of it.

Analysis: *Strike-Slip*

Type: Dramatic
Synopsis

A strike-slip is a fault rupture in which pieces of ground move parallel to each other, causing vibrations or shaking.

The play opens in a small market in downtown Los Angeles. Richmond has come in to buy some smokes and lottery tickets. Lee, the Korean owner, gives Richmond change. Richmond says he paid with a ten and a five. Lee says it was a ten and one. The two argue, and Richmond leaves with a threatening, "I'll be back."

Lee is the father of Angie. Richmond appears to be plotting something with Vince, to take revenge on Lee. Rafael's mother, Viviana, is a real estate agent and she's about to sell a very expensive home to a Caucasian couple, Dan and Rachel, in Santa Monica. Iizuka slowly unfolds a world in which race, status, and finances dictate how they experience the American dream.

No one is happy in the world. Viviane wants her son to grow up and be a successful businessman, unlike his father. Dan is having an affair with Vince. Richmond feels oppressed and disrespected.

Angie tries to steal money from her father's store to leave town, and he finds her. He slaps her repeatedly. Vince comes in and offers her money. She refuses him. Viviana finds Rafael packing his gun. She tells him if he takes it to never come back. Someone comes into the market and Lee shoots. Lee ends up in prison for shooting and killing someone.

Vince is in business with Richmond and has been skimming merchandise off the top for himself. Richmond knows this.

Rafael and Angie move in together. She is pregnant. Richmond ropes Rafael into his business. Rachel hits Angie in a car accident. Everyone is connected one way or another, and every move has an effect.

Character Description
Angie Lee, 17 years old
She's first-generation Korean American, born and raised in Los Angeles. Her boyfriend is Rafael, also seventeen years old. He is a second-generation Mexican American. Rafi says she hits like a guy, strong. Angie thinks she might want to be a doctor; a pediatrician. She believes that everyone has a plan for their life. She wants to be rich. She wants to get out, not out for the day to Santa Monica, but out and away. She's reading *Sister Carrie* by Theodore Dreiser. Angie doesn't remember her mother; she can look at her face in pictures, but it doesn't mean anything. She wants her father to speak English, not Korean.

Given Circumstances
Who are they? Rafael is Angie's boyfriend.
Where are they? A rooftop in downtown Los Angeles.
When does this take place? The present.
Why are they there? The couple is hanging out, watching traffic go by.
What is the pre-beat? Angie has been teaching Rafael Korean.

Questions
1. Can you state your objective in a simple, specific, and active way?
2. Whom are you talking to? Be specific and have a clear image.
3. Can you think of three adjectives to describe your character?
4. What can you see from this rooftop?
5. What attracts you most about Rafael?
6. Is he a good boyfriend?
7. Are you in love with him?
8. Why do you want/need to get out of town so badly?
9. What's your ideal life like?
10. What does it mean to be Korean American in Los Angeles?
11. What do you want to do with the rest of your life?

12. Angie considers stealing money from her dad in order to get out. Is this really an option?

13. Has she stolen before?

14. What is her home life like?

15. What's the urgency behind this monologue?

Appropriate
Branden Jacobs-Jenkins

CASSIDY

Do you know anything about cicadas?

Did you know they're the oldest bugs on earth? They only appear every thirteen years and these bugs outside—they're thirteen years old. I just realized . . . they're about as old as I am. But this is, like, the end of their life. They're about to die. Can you imagine if I just like died last year?

And do you know why they're singing?

It's because they're trying to find each other—to mate . . . But isn't it weird that they spend like all this time underground becoming teenagers, waiting to hatch, and then they just sing for a few weeks in the summer and then they die? This is like—this song is like the peak of their existence. Like the whole point of their lives is to be able to sing so that they can get with another cicada and then they die before their kids are even born?

And, also, how do baby cicadas learn the song? Is it just something that's programmed in them? Or maybe they just pick it up somewhere, listening when they're eggs. Maybe they're hearing it in their sleep, and that's how they learn? And their parents are dead, but they have this memory of a song that they think is a part of them?

I think I'm upset . . . See you in the morning.

Analysis: *Appropriate*

Type: Dramatic
Synopsis

It is summer in the South and the cicadas are everywhere. A family has converged on this small, rundown property because their father, Ray, has recently passed. It's up to the children to pack up, sell, or throw out the years of stuff inside and unload the house. This was formerly the family's summer house, but Ray moved into it permanently years ago. As is the case with most high-stake situations like this, fights break out often, and they're mean. The return of Frank, the black sheep of the family, now calling himself Franz, towing along a seemingly underage fiancée, doesn't help matters. This family defines dysfunction.

The estate is half a million dollars in debt. Toni plans on having an auction but has severely, in her brother Bo's eyes, mishandled everything. In fact, because of Toni, the sale of the house might put them even further in the red. The house is a major liability and a difficult sell, because there's an old family cemetery on the property.

As the family cleans out the house, horrible things are found. Ainsley discovers a photo album filled with photos of lynchings. Cassidy and Rhys discover jars of body parts in the study. Was Ray a racist and a murderer, or a collector of ephemera?

Although they try to hide the album from their children, everyone sees it. No one succeeds in throwing it out because it may be worth money. Franz, in a fury, and in an attempt to cleanse himself and his family, runs into the lake with the photos, pretty much destroying them.

Character Description
Cassidy, early teens

Cassidy is turning into quite a pretty young woman. She's finally getting her braces off. She goes to a dermatologist and wears contacts now. She posted photos to Facebook of her and her cousin Rhys at Ray's funeral. It is through Facebook that she has been talking to her uncle Frank, which is how he finds out about Ray's death, but she doesn't tell her parents about it. She's tired of people answering her questions with, "You'll understand when you're older." She was brought up to learn things, but no one will tell her anything.

Although she's been told not to, she spends an evening going through the photo album along with River, Frank's fiancée. Cassidy has the idea that the photos could be worth money.

Cassidy is fascinated by this side of the family, perhaps because she knows so little about it. Her mom's side of the family is boring. She likes to say, "I'm almost an adult" a lot.

Given Circumstances

Who are they? Rhys is Cassidy's cousin.
Where are they? Their grandfather's home in southeast Arkansas.
When does this take place? The present.
Why are they there? They are cleaning up the home before selling it.
What is the pre-beat? Cassidy was about to put the photo album in her aunt's car.

Questions

1. Can you state your objective in a simple, specific, and active way?
2. Whom are you talking to? Be specific and have a clear image.
3. Can you think of three adjectives to describe your character?
4. What does the house feel and smell like?
5. Are you attracted to Rhys?
6. How close have the two of you become over the past few days?
7. What have you discovered about your family since arriving?
8. Can you describe the sound of the cicadas?
9. How do you know so much about the insect?

10. What do you think about the pictures you've seen?
11. Do you think your grandfather was a racist?
12. Do you think you are racist?
13. Has race played a part in your life up to this point?
14. Do you know your parents are having financial problems?
15. What's the urgency behind this monologue?

Don't Talk, Don't See
Julie Jensen

WANDA

I own these phones. Me and Danny own em. We charge people use em, cuz a lot of business goes on outta here. 7-Eleven, across the street from the El Cortez? Think about it. People that don't want their cell phone number known. That's who uses these phones. We charge a buck use the phone. Sometimes five, depends.

See, way it happened, I'm waiting for Danny. Like now. This guy comes up to me. Says he give me ten bucks I stay right where I am next fifteen minutes. I do it. He pays me. So whenever I'm hanging out down here, I do same thing. Sit here. Collect. Pack a cigarettes. You know.

Sometimes he talks to me. I like how he talks. Can't hardly hear him.

Job is I'm here, like a signal. He makes a call, leaves the drop, then cuts. Someone picks up drop. And I got quick ten. So now I got two jobs. I got this job for him and I got the phones. Score twenty bucks half an hour.

Danny's been in house for a week, some guy beat his face. Danny likes it dangerous. Picks up trash. I tell him, you know, I tell him. But he's 14 now, can't hear.

Danny says the end of the earth already happened. When they blew the last underground bomb. Says cracked the earth and stuff is running out now, radioactive. All over everything.

Once you believe that, you got a certain way of living. Like Danny. Scared of nothing. Cuz you already dead.

Analysis: *Don't Talk, Don't See*

Type: Dramatic
Synopsis and Character Description

This monologue comes from a slightly longer monologue that was part of Humana Festival's 2006 collection of plays and monologues performed under the title *Neon Mirage*.

Wanda is fourteen years old. She is sitting on a newspaper stand in front of a 7-Eleven. There is a line of pay phones behind her. Wanda has many piercings and looks like a goth girl. She smokes. She is talking to an unseen girl, trying to scare her and enjoying it.

The audience knows nothing of Wanda outside of what is in this monologue. It's up to the actor playing the role to decide who Danny is and what he looks like, along with the details of their relationship. Wanda's use of language tells you a lot about her personality, but whether she chooses to speak that way or was raised speaking that way is a choice you need to make.

Obviously, being fourteen years old means money is very important to her. If this story about the man is true, she has the potential to make a lot of money. The reference to the end of the earth and the radio-activity is a sudden revelation. If it's true, it places Wanda under even greater stakes.

Wanda repeats the phrase "Don't talk, don't see" throughout the piece. She's scared. This job she has is very dangerous. As the piece progresses, she hears the sounds of sirens approaching. Danny never appears. The girl Wanda is speaking to runs away and Wanda is left alone and scared. Suddenly the police are there and the play is over.

Given Circumstances

Who are they? Wanda is speaking to a girl about her age.

Where are they? By the 7-Eleven phone booths.

When does this take place? The present.

Why are they there? Wanda is working.

What is the pre-beat? This is the beginning of the scene.

Questions

1. Can you state your objective in a simple, specific, and active way?
2. Whom are you talking to? Be specific and have a clear image.
3. Can you think of three adjectives to describe your character?
4. Is this girl you're speaking to a friend, or an enemy?
5. How long have you been working these phones?
6. How did you discover you could make money doing this?
7. How much money do you need to make a day in order to survive?
8. How long have you and Danny been friends?
9. What does he look like?
10. How do you split the proceeds?
11. What does this guy who just came up look like?
12. What do you spend your money on?
13. Do you want this girl to stay with you for company?
14. Do you have any other friends?
15. Are you scared you'll get in trouble or get hurt?

Chronicles Simpkins Will Cut Your Ass
Rolin Jones

JESSICA

You can't do that, Mr. Finkel. There's a context for things.

She'll be expelled. Principal Cody will ship her to another school and she'll rule the tetherball court there and all the same jealousies will conspire to break her spirit. Pretty soon she'll be selling her body for crack. Is that what you want? You want Chronicles smoking crack? You want her to ruin her life? Did you run out here to this small little bit of asphalt, blowing your whistle, making wild accusations because you're trying to justify your existence, Mr. Finkel?

Because you have failed to prepare your students, students like Billy Conn for the coming world? A world that is surprising, and scary and yes, occasionally unfair? It's something he can't find in the books you make us read. And the lessons you draw on the chalkboard.

You have to let children fall, Mr. Finkel. You have to let them fall and get back up on their own. Chronicles is an outcast here, Mr. Finkel. In exile everywhere she carries her Fun Dip. But from ten-thirty to one-fifteen she feels safe. When Chronicles steps into this circle, when she's hitting her high arcing serves, and flying that ball over the heads of children more privileged than her, for a brief moment in space and time, Mr. Finkel. Chronicles Simpkins is immortal. And just witnessing it is a thing of beauty. And you want to take that away from her. From us. Shame on you, Mr. Finkel.

Analysis: *Chronicles Simpkins Will Cut Your Ass*

Type: Seriocomic
Synopsis and Character Description

The play opens with three fourth-grade girls playing tetherball at recess. Chronicles, Rachel, and Jessica are in the school playground. Jessica has little coordination, an iPhone, and a huge, burdensome backpack.

Chronicles and Rachel are tougher girls than Jessica. They have attitude. Chronicles and Rachel talk smack about other kids in the playground and threaten them, as well. Any infraction, however small, can provoke their wrath. Jessica has a watch and it's her job to keep time. When Chronicles hears something she doesn't like, she'll threaten to cut your ass. And even though she doesn't have a knife, she can do it with the rope and ball she's playing tetherball with.

Billy Conn challenges her to a game. Rachel explains that Chronicles is the "Woodlake Avenue Elementary Recess, Lunch and After School Undisputed Unified Tetherball Champion." She's won seventy-eight games in a row. Chronicles wins by pepper-spraying Billy in the face and temporarily blinding him.

The principal storms in and demands that Chronicles admit she did it. He says Billy is in with the nurse and an ambulance is on the way. This is not the first time Chronicles has struck. As he begins to pull Chronicles into the building, Jessica jumps to her defense.

Chronicles uses the distraction to suddenly lift up her shirt and put the principal's hands on her boobs while Rachel snaps a picture. She gets out of trouble and she gets her pepper spray back.

Jessica wears headgear and takes it off for this monologue. She perhaps has a slight lisp when she speaks.

They go back to playing tetherball.

Given Circumstances

Who are they? Mr. Finkel is a teacher.

Where are they? The school playground.

When does this take place? The present.

Why are they there? It's recess and Chronicles is causing trouble.

What is the pre-beat? Mr. Finkel is about to drag Chronicles to the principal's office.

Questions

1. Can you state your objective in a simple, specific, and active way?
2. Can you think of three adjectives to describe your character?
3. Is Mr. Finkel one of your teachers?
4. Do you like/respect him?
5. How old would he say he is?
6. What does Chronicles look like?
7. How long have you been friends with her?
8. Are you friends with her because you like her, or because you're scared of her?
9. How many people has she threatened and/or hurt in the time you've known her?
10. Do you often speak up for yourself or other people?
11. Would you consider yourself a good student?
12. Is it exciting to hang out with Chronicles?
13. What's the urgency behind this monologue?
14. What grade are you in?
15. Who is Billy Conn, and what does he look like?

Unlikely Jihadist
Michael Kimmel

CYNTHIA

This is stupid. Really. Stupid.

It's just twitter. Nobody takes it seriously.

One time, Jenny Simmons (who I don't even know well), she goes to my school, tweeted that Mr. Shapely had herpes. And NOBODY LISTENED. Cause its twitter. And it's stupid.

Does my Dad know I'm here? Does he know why? Did he call his lawyer? Shouldn't I have one? A lawyer?

This is insane. I DIDN'T EVEN DO ANYTHING.

Tommy Flanders, he's one of those trench coat kids, total psycho, posted on Facebook that he was looking up how to make explosives, and, like, nothing happened to him. They just got him a counselor, and searched his locker, but he was totally faking.

STUPID.

How did American Airlines even read it? NOBODY follows me. I was just bored, and nothing was on TV, and I was, like, watching these jihad videos . . .

DADDY????

Is this rendition? Am I at a black site? I completely saw Zero Dark Thirty. Are you gonna put me in a box? Play death metal until I crack?

Am I considered a terrorist?

Does my mom know? Did the school call her? She's at some function.

They expelled a girl. Last year. She had been tweeting at this freak show in our grade, and they called it harassment. Bullying. She's home schooled now.

If I'm arrested, can I still get my license? I'm supposed to get my permit. Like, really soon.

It was dumb. I know that. But I got all these retweets and followers from it. It felt cool. For like, a minute.

It just seemed funny. At the time. Really funny. And then everyone was talking about it . . .

Is my dad coming? Can I call him? Talk to him?

I'm not a jihadist. I just, I felt famous for a second. Did you see the responses?

I'm sorry. For doing it. I should have been doing my homework . . .

Another kid, Spencer, sent a picture of his thing to Sophia. And then it got sent around. So they put all the kids in school in the auditorium. To tell us not to send pictures of ourselves to each other.

I didn't think anyone would take me seriously. I don't really want to blow up a plane.

Can I go home now?

Analysis: *Unlikely Jihadist*

Type: Seriocomic
Synopsis and Character Description

This piece was written as a stand-alone monologue, so all of the factual information you need about the character and events can be found within.

Cynthia is a high school student who, judging, by her language and behavior, could be anywhere between the ages of fifteen and seventeen. She obviously has tweeted a threat against a plane that, in this day and age, was taken very seriously. She is now in the hands of police or government officials who are trying to determine what exactly her intentions are.

She must be utterly terrified to be alone and under such close scrutiny in an undisclosed location. The fact that she asks for a lawyer—her father's lawyer—leads me to believe she comes from a family of some affluence. She also seems like a privileged girl who gets what she wants. Cynthia says she's about to get her driver's permit, which means a license, which means a car.

Also pay attention to her point of view when she speaks of other kids at her school. For example, Tommy Flanders is a "trench coat kid," a "total psycho." These words are spoken by someone who seems to be getting through high school on the popular side, or at least the not-bullied side.

Over and over again Cynthia calls for her father. He must be the one who rescues her in any emergency. She barely mentions her mother, but you must have an idea and an understanding of how both of those relationships function as a unit as well as separately.

Finally, it's important to note how long it takes for Cynthia to apologize. She doesn't appear to be someone who takes responsibility for her actions all that often. In this case, under extreme circumstances, she finally does it.

This is a highly difficult monologue to pull off. You must carefully calibrate the journey of a girl who goes from being entitled and scared to being truly vulnerable and scared. Cynthia has the facade of a "mean girl," but underneath she knows that she has royally screwed up and even her father and her lawyers aren't going to be of any help. Her eventual acceptance of the act and apology for it is, most likely, a huge (and rare) step for her.

Given Circumstances

Who are they? Cynthia is talking to a government official, perhaps an FBI agent.

Where are they? A cold, unfriendly office or cell.

When does this take place? The present.

Why are they there? Cynthia tweeted a potential threat against her school.

What is the pre-beat? Cynthia has been arrested.

Questions

1. Can you state your objective in a simple, specific, and active way?
2. Whom are you talking to? Be specific and have a clear image.
3. Can you think of three adjectives to describe your character?
4. Can you describe the room you're in?
5. When during the monologue do you really become scared?
6. Would you consider yourself a good student?
7. Do you get into trouble often?
8. What does your father look like?
9. Does he often rush to your aid when you need it?
10. What exactly did you tweet?
11. How great was it to be popular and funny because of it?
12. How big is your school?
13. How many friends do you have there?
14. Do you think this will affect your entire future?
15. What's your mother going to say?
16. What's the urgency behind this monologue?

Henry's Law
Stacie Lents

ANNIE

Do you know what my least favorite part of school is?

Attendance. At the beginning of the year. I'm "B," so I don't have to wait too long, you know. Abernathy, Robert; Alvarez, Lia; Anders, Allison; Anderson, Jamila; Atkins, William; Bart, Christopher; Bernstein—any relation to Max?

As far as the teachers at Clearview go, that's basically my first name—for the first couple of weeks anyway . . . "Any relation to Max" Bernstein. Oh don't get me wrong. They eventually learn my name. And once they figure out I'm stupid, once I get my first C, they pretty much leave me alone. It's only those first few weeks that I'm "Max's sister"—where they're calling on me when my hand isn't even in the air like the wrong answer I gave 10 minutes ago must have been a mistake. But it's the first second right after "Bernstein" that I just want to bash their stupid faces in: "Any relation to Max."

How can you not know it? You've seen your report card. A, A, A, A, A, A, A, A. It's like even your report card is screaming "AAAAHHHHHHHHHHHH."

Analysis: *Henry's Law*

Type: Seriocomic
Synopsis

Max and Annie are siblings. Max, about seventeen years old, is the older brother. He's far from cool. In fact, he's kind of a science nerd. He conducts experiments in his bedroom. Annie, fifteen years old and a freshman, wants to be popular and isn't exactly proud about living in her older brother's geeky shadow. In the first scene, we learn that Max is preparing to tutor Sara Culverson, a popular kid and the girlfriend of Jason Swarthmore. Annie, who has been trying to teach him how to flirt, tells him that flirting is in fact useless with Sara because she's out of his league.

The first tutoring session takes place in Sara's bedroom, and it's awkward. Max misidentifies an Usher poster as Justin Bieber and is just generally awkward. But the two finally find some common ground and get to work.

Sara comes to Max's house for another study session. After Annie does a lengthy photo shoot with Sara for her Facebook page, Max and Annie get to talking. Sara finds herself attracted to Max and kisses him. Annie walks in and sees this. The next day at school, Annie finds Jason and tells him she saw Sara kissing another boy. Jason loses it.

An online viral smear campaign against Max, falsely outing him as a homosexual, begins. It seems like Jason is the one behind it. Annie is most worried about how the scandal will affect her.

Max stops returning Sara's calls and even stops going to school. Max kills himself. He purchases arsenic online and takes it. Jason is ostracized at school. Everyone blames him for Max's suicide. When he goes to Sara for comfort, she admits that she was the one who started the online rumors because Max wouldn't respond to her advances.

Character Description
Annie Bernstein, 14–15years old
Annie is a freshman at Clearview High School. She wants to help Max, her brother, become more popular. She tries, unsuccessfully, to teach him how to flirt. Max embarrasses her. Annie wants to be popular. Max is the opposite, and everyone knows that they're related. She freaks out when she learns whom Max is tutoring. Sara is popular because she's dating Jason "Sexy" Swarthmore. Annie misuses the word *hypothetically* often. Max constantly corrects her. She's on a dance committee at school, either Homecoming or Spring Fling. It's only when Max dies that Annie realizes what a good brother he was and all the things she'll miss by not having him around.

Given Circumstances
Who are they? Annie is talking to her older brother, Max.

Where are they? Max has locked himself in his room, Annie is in the hall.

When does this take place? The present.

Why are they there? Rumors about Max being homosexual have been circulating around school.

What is the pre-beat? Max just referenced their social status at school.

Questions
1. Can you state your objective in a simple, specific, and active way?
2. Whom are you talking to? Be specific and have a clear image.
3. Can you think of three adjectives to describe your character?
4. Do you and Max look alike?
5. Are you jealous of how smart he is?
6. What does it mean to you to be popular?
7. Do you feel badly about telling Jason you saw Max kiss Sara?
8. If so, where do you feel that guilt in your body?

9. Do you think you're responsible for Max's ostracism?
10. What does Jason look like?
11. What does Sara look like?
12. How do you see yourself in comparison to them?
13. Do you wish you could take all of this back?
14. How big is your school?
15. What can you do to make Max feel better about himself?

All Hail Hurricane Gordo
Carly Mensch

INDIA

I don't have a license.

I live in Manhattan. No one knows how to drive there.

I want you to drive yourself across the country, and bring me with you. I'm really fun to travel with. I promise. Like really, really fun. And I'm a master at the radio. I can even find radio stations you never even knew existed. The stations *in between* the stations.

We're like, the same. We're both kinda stuck I guess.

That's what I always said. Back home, sitting on my bed. *I could leave whenever I want; I could just get up and walk out.* And then, about a year ago, I just started doing it. Getting up and leaving right in the middle of things. Like if I was watching a movie and it was absolutely god-awful, I'd just get up and leave. Or if I was having dinner with a bunch of friends and the conversation just sounded like empty white noise gossip talk, I'd just get up and go eat by myself. Because life is short, right? We're all going to die so we might as well do what we want while we're here. That's what all the philosophers tell you. All those dead French guys. And look—they're dead, right? So they must have been on to something. I guess I'm kind of cobbling together my world-view as I go along. Right now I'm in a very dead French guy/James Dean outlaw place. But tomorrow—who knows? Right?

Analysis: *All Hail Hurricane Gordo*

Type: Seriocomic
Synopsis

The action of the play takes place in the living room of a suburban New York house that has been converted into a makeshift office.

Chaz and Gordo and brothers in their twenties. They work together out of their home. They are a modern-day odd couple. Chaz is up, dressed, and working every morning at 9:30 a.m. Gordo can't even put his pants on. They argue and wrestle like children. Chaz has to give Gordo time-outs. Chaz thinks Gordo has anger-management issues.

They are in a financial crisis. Gordo can't hold down a job and, according to Chaz, has majorly messed up his chances at ever landing one again. Chaz has sold their TV. Today they are interviewing a possible tenant.

India arrives for the interview. She doesn't like answering personal questions and turns things around by interviewing Chaz. Gordo comes out and kicks India out of his chair. He explains that he's the creative genius between the two brothers. Chaz asks India if she'll take the room. She says yes and pays in cash.

Gordo tells India that Chaz has so many phone books because he writes letters, hundreds of letters, to people. But he won't tell her what the letters are for or about. Gordo bangs his head on the desk repeatedly in front of India and it freaks her out. He tells her he needs discipline. Gordo is afraid Child Protective Services will come and take him away.

Oscar, India's father, shows up and India runs into her bedroom and shuts the door. Oscar says that she planned all this, meaning his arrival and her refusal to see him. Oscar is here to bring India back to reality. He takes a liking to Chaz. Oscar owns a string of sporting goods stores and could maybe help Chaz with a job.

India won't go home with her father. He leaves her there to think about what she's doing and what she wants. His pet rabbit, Bob, is missing, but she denies having it. She smuggled it in her French horn case. Chaz admits the letters he writes are to people all over the country asking if they're related to him. He wants a family. India says she's not going home. India gives Bob to Gordo to take care of. She goes to leave, and Chaz decides to go with her, leaving Gordo on his own.

Character Description
India, 18 years old
India is a self-styled rebel with a blue streak in her hair. She likes Orangina. She's a musician. She used to play the French horn. She likes a movie called *The Devils* starring Vanessa Redgrave that's akin to a gothic porno. She has very little money right now, so $500 rent is an amazing deal. She thought the house would be seedier. She doesn't want Chaz asking her any personal questions in the interview because this is more a financial arrangement to her. She doesn't like the service sector of the economy. She thinks people waiting on other people is demeaning. She lies and says she twenty-four. She wants to live here even though she finds the place creepy like an Edgar Allan Poe story. It's the ambiguity and the threat of danger that attracts her. She has a yellow belt in tae kwon do. She's an only child.

Given Circumstances
Who are they? Chaz is India's landlord.
Where are they? The living room of Chaz's house.
When does this take place? The present.
Why are they there? India has run away from home and is renting a room here.
What is the pre-beat? Chaz tells India he assumed she thought him awkward and boring.

Questions

1. Can you state your objective in a simple, specific, and active way?
2. Whom are you talking to? Be specific and have a clear image.
3. Can you think of three adjectives to describe your character?
4. You haven't known Chaz for all that long. Are you ready to road-trip with him?
5. You tell a lot of lies. Why?
6. What's your real home life like, with your mom and dad?
7. Why did you run away?
8. Have you contacted your parents at all since leaving?
8. Whose money are you using to pay the rent?
9. What is this household like?
10. Do you like Chaz and Gordo?
11. Do you like living away from home?
12. Is it difficult living in a suburb and not the city?
13. Are you attracted to Chaz?
14. What does he look like?
15. Besides dead French guys and James Dean, who else has shaped your worldview, and why?

girl.
Megan Mostyn-Brown

HANNAH

My mom hasn't said anything all day.

I take that back.

She hasn't said anything to me.

She said thank you to the police officer who came to the house.

And she mumbled Lizzie's name to the receptionist at the morgue.

I didn't go in.

I sat in a plastic chair in the hallway and counted the number of

tiles on the floor from my feet to the front desk.

There are seventy-two.

They didn't have any pamphlets to read,

which was really surprising

because like every place in the hospital has at least

One

Pamphlet

But,

what would the morgue have pamphlets about?

Anyway,

I'm glad I didn't go in with mom,

you know,

to look at the body and stuff.

Because

when people drown they get all

blue and bloated

not like I've ever seen it
but
that's what happens in movies.
I'd like to think of Lizzie like
that picture,
the one of Ophelia,
I don't remember who painted it
but
it's Ophelia floating on her back in this pond
and
she's wearing a really beautiful dress with a crown of flowers
on her head.
That's how I'd like to think of her.

Analysis: *girl.*

Type: Dramatic
Synopsis and Character Description
This monologue is from Part I of *girl* and it's titled "Things You Can't Tell Just by Looking at Her."

Hannah is fifteen years old. She dresses simply, no makeup or jewelry. She could be any girl from any high school. She is someone you wouldn't take special note of if you saw her on the street.

Hannah's sister Lizzie died today. Lizzie has always been trouble, running away all the time. Hannah and her mom never spoke about Lizzie absences, but they were more than noticeable. Hannah feels bad because she hasn't cried over the death. All she can think about is the fact that if she was going to commit suicide, she wouldn't do it on a Monday in July. She would do it in a cold, rainy month so that people would wonder: "did she do it on purpose or did she slip?"

Other things Hannah thinks about while sitting in the hospital waiting room: she and her mom will be the only people at Lizzie's funeral because they have no idea who Lizzie's friends are, and she'll have to buy a short-sleeved black dress for the funeral because it's so hot out. Hannah makes no mention of her father.

It was common knowledge that Lizzie was a drug addict. Hannah also heard rumors that Lizzie would have sex with people for money. Hannah remembers a night she took care of Lizzie after some guy kicked her out of his car and threw her on the lawn.

Hannah has two friends, Janie and Marie, but they're not very close and neither one has called her to find out how she is.

Hannah cuts herself. She has marks all over her arms. She's been cutting for two years. She has also cut words into her legs: "hate" and "ugly." She started cutting because her mother never really had time for her. No one was ever around to recognize her accomplishments. Her mother was always out looking for Lizzie or dealing with Lizzie's problems. Hannah ultimately took on the role of mother in the house, and it became too much to handle.

Given Circumstances

Who are they? Hannah is talking to the audience.

Where are they? She could be anywhere: her bedroom, the hospital, et cetera.

When does this take place? The present.

Why are they there? Her sister has just died.

What is the pre-beat? She was just thinking about how she'd commit suicide if she were to do so.

Questions

1. What did Lizzie look like?
2. Where do you feel her in your body when you think about her?

3. What lessons did you learn from her while she was alive?

4. What does your mom look like?

5. Were you with her when she got the news about Lizzie ?

6. What's your favorite memory of you and Lizzie?

7. What class did you read *Hamlet* for?

8. What exactly is the image of Ophelia you're talking about?

9. Do you think Lizzie killed herself?

10. Are you tired of mothering?

11. Where do you make the cuts on your body?

12. How do you hide them?

13. What else are you hiding?

14. Do you do well in school?

15. What do you want to be when you're older?

girl.
Megan Mostyn-Brown

LUCY

I mean I just look like myself.

But yeah—

See

I stand in front of the mirror in the bathroom at school

girls in front of me swiping off layers of lip gloss

mascara

adjusting their special Victoria's Secrets bras.

Shit,

I don't even wear a bra half the time.

And I wouldn't know what to do with a bag of make-up if you

fuckin' hit me with it.

It's like once

my mom won these tickets for a free meal at this Italian restaurant

in Geneva

you know the kind where they got forks for

like

every course.

So my mom

not like she had ever done this

but

she made me dress up.

Pantyhose,

coral pink lipstick,

this powder blue dress from the Fashion Bug

and some low heels
and
I made a fuckin' royal stink about it.
Yellin'
and everything.
But secretly,
I was a little excited
to ya' know
see what I looked like.
So I fixed myself in the bathroom mirror
and
I looked good
really good
but I didn't look like
me.

Analysis: *girl.*

Type: Dramatic
Synopsis and Character Description

This monologue is from Part II of *girl* and it's titled "We Did What We Could with What We Had."

Lucy is seventeen years old. Isaac perhaps describes her best when he says that she's like an avocado: tough skin, soft on the inside, with a strong core. Lucy lives in a very small Midwestern town. She's youthful and sassy, but she's seen a lot. She stands outside alone at night with a large duffel bag and an atlas. This short plays is told through alternating monologues by Lucy, her mother, and Isaac.

Lucy's mother is in her early thirties. She's been a waitress and a bartender for years. Lucy has always stood out. Lucy's dad left right after she was born and they've never met.

Lucy doesn't dress like a boy, but she has a penchant for oversized, baggy clothes, and she wears boys' hightop sneakers.

Lucy and Isaac have been friends since the ninth grade. Isaac was immediately taken with the girl who skateboarded to school, camera around her neck, and had few friends. He admires her bravery in being who she is. They're not really boyfriend and girlfriend, but they are very close.

Lucy has only ever kissed one boy. She was twelve years old, and he was the son of a friend of her mother. Other than that, she is a virgin. Isaac overhears her lying to a group of girls about the strangest place she's ever had sex. He pulls her aside and tells her she shouldn't disrespect herself like that. That's how they became friends. She badly wants to kiss Isaac but never has. He did spend the entire night with her once, holding her hand all night long, but nothing more happened.

Lucy is unhappy here. She wants to leave town, get away from everything and everyone, and go somewhere where she can be herself without anyone judging her. Isaac also wants to leave—even before graduation. He plans to steal his dad's Firebird and drive into the sun until they hit the ocean. Lucy barely thinks twice about it. She wants to go. She packs her duffel bag with the items she needs and waits.

Isaac is sitting in his car thinking about whether or not to actually go through with the plan.

Given Circumstances

Who are they? Lucy is talking to the audience.
Where are they? She is standing on a street corner.
When does this take place? The present, 1:00 a.m.

Why are they there? She is waiting for Isaac to pick her up.

What is the pre-beat? Lucy said people think she looks like a boy.

Questions

1. What does Lucy see when she looks in the mirror?
2. What part of herself does she like the most?
3. What would she like to change?
4. What does her mom look like?
5. Where does she feel her mom in her body when she thinks about her?
6. Does she want to make her mom happy?
7. What does Isaac look like?
8. Where does she feel Isaac in her body when she thinks about him?
9. How badly does she need to get out of this town?
10. What will be different in California?
11. Is Lucy in love with Isaac?
12. Does she want to kiss him more?
13. Does she want to lose her virginity to him?
14. Does she have any other friends?
15. What's the urgency in this monologue?

Franny's Way
Richard Nelson

DOLLY

I can't even remember the show. As soon as the lights went down,
I guess so Grandma couldn't see or do anything to stop us, Mom
reached over and took my hand and held it in hers.

Then she pulled it to her, and pressed it against her chest.
Then she kissed it. I put my head against her shoulder. She
stroked my head. She touched my cheek. I looked up at her. We
cried throughout the whole play.

At the intermission, Mom went outside to smoke a cigarette.
Grandma tried to buy me some candy, but I just followed Mom.
Grandma said something about how "you haven't given up that
awful habit, have you Jennifer?" The cigarettes.

Grandma wanted me to go inside with her, but I wouldn't.
Then Mom snapped open her purse—with thin gold stripes and
a gold band—.

And took out a photo. And said here, Dolly, this is "my man."

That's what she said, called him—"my man." Grandma made
this awful sound and sort of ran away—for an instant, 'cause she
was back in a second, but not before I had a chance to look . . .
Back inside, she slipped it into my hand, and I hid it in my
program.

Analysis: *Franny's Way*

Type: Seriocomic
Synopsis

The action of the play takes place in New York City's Greenwich Village in 1957. It is summer, and hot. The apartment belongs to Sally and her husband, Phil. The play opens with the couple discovering their baby girl dead in her crib. The doctors called it "crib death."

Franny and Dolly, live in Millbrook, New York with their father and his new wife. Marjorie, the grandmother of the three girls, decides to take them on a trip to the city. Franny doesn't really care about Sally's sorrow. She is coming to visit her boyfriend, who attends NYU. Dolly has secretly arranged a meeting with her mother.

The women arrive approximately six weeks after the baby's death. Franny (seventeen) and Dolly (fifteen) are surprised at how small the apartment is and that the bathroom is in the hallway, and shared among tenants.

Things between Sally and Phil are very tense at the moment. They try to present the picture of a happy couple on the surface, but underneath, they are losing the ability to communicate. Sally breaks out in tears from time to time. Phil steers the conversation in another direction when this happens.

Franny gets stood up by her boyfriend. She calls to find out here he is and he tells her he's met someone else. She vomits all over herself in a phone booth.

Dolly comes home flushed and excited from meeting with her mother at Gimbels. She, her grandmother, and her mother had lunch together and then went to *My Fair Lady*. Franny and Sally have an argument. Sally says she sees right through Franny's "grown-up" act. In an attempt to get back at Sally, Franny makes a sexual pass at Phil.

He rejects her and then goes into the bedroom and sleeps with Sally for the first time in months.

The women return to Millbrook and life goes on. The play, narrated by Older Franny, is about how the fragility of life isn't apparent to us until we're older. The young are oblivious.

Character Description
Dolly, 15 years old

Dolly has never been to the city before. She organized tickets to see *My Fair Lady* on Broadway. Dolly's father paid, of course, but Dolly had to write away for them and organize all the details. Dolly has noticeably grown in the past few months. This is the first summer she didn't take her sheep to the Dutchess County Fair. She's growing up in every way. Dolly doesn't understand why Sally breaks into tears. She stands at the window and watches the action on the street, fascinated. Dolly has seen Franny stand in the mirror and just stare at herself. She wants to visit Gimbels department store before going to the theater.

Given Circumstances
Who are they? Franny is Dolly's older sister.
Where are they? Their cousin Sally's Greenwich Village apartment.
When does this take place? August 1957.
Why are they there? To cheer up Sally and Phil after the death of their baby.
What is the pre-beat? Franny asks Dolly if she believed their mother actually wrote them letters after leaving.

Questions
1. Can you state your objective in a simple, specific, and active way?
2. Whom are you talking to? Be specific and have a clear image.
3. Can you think of three adjectives to describe your character?

4. How long ago did your mother leave?
5. Do you miss her?
6. How often do you get to talk to her?
7. Were you scared she wouldn't show up for your meeting?
8. Was this meeting difficult to plan?
9. Does Franny remind you of your mother?
10. What is *My Fair Lady* about?
11. Why did you choose that musical to go see?
12. Why didn't you include Franny in these plans?
13. Are you angry with you mother for leaving?
14. Was this your first Broadway show?
15. How did spending this afternoon with your mom make you feel?

Franny's Way
Richard Nelson

DOLLY

I had gotten her number out of Dad's desk. There's a—divorce file. You know Father, he's so—(Organized).

I knew it was there. And I found it and I called her and I told her because she'd really really want to know that I got the part of the young girl in *Our Hearts Were Young and Gay*. I thought she'd really want to know about my costume. Because she always made our costumes with us for Halloween. So . . .

And she couldn't wait to see me in the play, she said. I didn't ask her, I didn't make her, it's just what she said. (*Beat*) And then she wasn't there.

But she *did* come. And she asked me if I liked her flowers. I never got any flowers. Did I?

Remember the little boy playing the steward on the ship? And how he came on stage all proud and was supposed to be saying: "All ashore who's going ashore!" but instead shouted: "All aboard who's going ashore." And then cried? (*Beat*) Mom said that was her favorite part. I hadn't said anything about it, she told me . . . Her favorite—except of course for me.

Analysis: *Franny's Way*

Type: Seriocomic
Synopsis

The action of the play takes place in New York City's Greenwich Village in 1957. It is summer, and hot. The apartment belongs to Sally and her husband, Phil. The play opens with the couple discovering their baby girl dead in her crib. The doctors called it "crib death."

Franny and Dolly, live in Millbrook, New York with their father and his new wife. Marjorie, the grandmother of the three girls, decides to take them on a trip to the city. Franny doesn't really care about Sally's sorrow. She is coming to visit her boyfriend, who attends NYU. Dolly has secretly arranged a meeting with her mother.

The women arrive approximately six weeks after the baby's death. Franny (seventeen) and Dolly (fifteen) are surprised at how small the apartment is and that the bathroom is in the hallway, and shared among tenants.

Things between Sally and Phil are very tense at the moment. They try to present the picture of a happy couple on the surface, but underneath, they are losing the ability to communicate. Sally breaks out in tears from time to time. Phil steers the conversation in another direction when this happens.

Franny gets stood up by her boyfriend. She calls to find out here he is and he tells her he's met someone else. She vomits all over herself in a phone booth.

Dolly comes home flushed and excited from meeting with her mother at Gimbels. She, her grandmother, and her mother had lunch together and then went to *My Fair Lady*. Franny and Sally have an argument. Sally says she sees right through Franny's "grown-up" act. In an attempt to get back at Sally, Franny makes a sexual pass at Phil.

He rejects her and then goes into the bedroom and sleeps with Sally for the first time in months.

The women return to Millbrook and life goes on. The play, narrated by Older Franny, is about how the fragility of life isn't apparent to us until we're older. The young are oblivious.

Character Description
Dolly, 15 years old
Dolly has never been to the city before. She organized tickets to see *My Fair Lady* on Broadway. Dolly's father paid, of course, but Dolly had to write away for them and organize all the details. Dolly has noticeably grown in the past few months. This is the first summer she didn't take her sheep to the Dutchess County Fair. She's growing up in every way. Dolly doesn't understand why Sally breaks into tears. She stands at the window and watches the action on the street, fascinated. Dolly has seen Franny stand in the mirror and just stare at herself. She wants to visit Gimbels department store before going to the theater.

Given Circumstances
Who are they? Franny is Dolly's older sister.
Where are they? Their cousin Sally's Greenwich Village apartment.
When does this take place? August 1957.
Why are they there? To cheer up Sally and Phil after the death of their baby.
What is the pre-beat? Franny asks Dolly how she found her mother's number.

Questions
1. Can you state your objective in a simple, specific, and active way?
2. Whom are you talking to? Be specific and have a clear image.
3. Can you think of three adjectives to describe your character?

4. Was it difficult arranging this meeting with your mother?
5. When is the last time you saw her? What were the circumstances?
6. Do you miss her?
7. Where in your body do you feel her when you think about her?
8 Does Franny remind you of your mother?
9. Did you feel guilty sneaking behind your father's back?
10. Is this your first trip to New York City?
11. What are you learning here?
12. What does "divorce" mean to you?
13. Do your friends have divorced parents?
14. Why did you choose *My Fair Lady* as the show to see?
15. Was it difficult not telling anyone of your plan?

Edith Can Shoot Things and Hit Them
A. Rey Pamatmat

EDITH

I am very mature for my age. It's true, Fergie, I am. I look twelve, but I'm really much, much older. Everyone says so.

Who cares what you believe? The truth is true. Our kind mature at a different speed than stupid, little human girls. On my planet, I'm a full-grown grown-up, and I have my own apartment where I live without my twenty parents. Who needs them?

Yeah! Twenty people to build one baby, and they all get together to help the baby grow. Feed her and make her clothes and paint her bedroom a different color every month no matter how expensive it is. There's always someone around, because everyone has twenty parents.

But that was when I was small. Now I'm stuck here, alone on this planet as a test. To see—well, I don't know, but it's a test. THAT'S the test: for me to figure out what the test is. And I've got to do it fast, before the evil shape-changing aliens from an enemy planet take over our world!

And Kenny waits to see if I complete the test, which is how he'll know I'm ready to fight in the war. And when I am, I'll sprout wings and fly away! My kind have wings when they grow up.

Well, I mean, I'm a grown up now, but when I grow up more, I'll fly away and return to my planet, shoot those aliens in their faces, save Kenny's life, and rescue my twenty parents, who are really, actually helpless without me.

And I'm going to do it all by myself.

Analysis: *Edith Can Shoot Things and Hit Them*

Type: Seriocomic
Synopsis

Edith and Kenny, her brother, live with their father on a remote piece of property far from town. There is a house, a barn, and an orchard. Edith has very few friends but a very vivid imagination. She sits in the eaves of the barn with a pellet gun and dreams of being a "big, grown-up girl."

Edith and Kenny have a rough relationship with their father. He's mostly absent, preferring to stay at his girlfriend's house. He forgets to put money in the bank that they need for food and gas. Kenny spends most of his free time at his friend Benji's house. The mother of one of Edith's friends will call from time to time to check in and make sure Edith is eating the right things. Edith, tired of being alone all the time, tells Kenny to make Benji come over to their house. This small event precipitates a lot of action: Benji kisses Kenny while Edith does homework in the other room; Kenny and Benji go into the barn and begin a sexual relationship since there are no adults around. Kenny finds the nerve to call his dad and demand money.

Kenny and Benji carry on their relationship as secretly as possible. Kenny doesn't want anyone to find out their dad isn't there, because then the state would split Edith and him apart. Benji's mom, however, finds out about the relationship and does not handle it well. Benji moves in with Edith and Kenny.

Edith hears a noise late one night and shoots the pellet gun out the window. She ends up hitting Chloe, her dad's girlfriend, who has to go to the hospital and have a pellet removed from her shoulder. As punishment, Edith's father sends her to a private Catholic reform school. She escapes, and Kenny once again threatens their father into letting Edith stay under Kenny's "custody."

Character Description
Edith, almost 13 years old

Edith is a Filipino-American whose mother has passed away, and she lives with her brother. She has a giant stuffed frog named Fergie. She is in choir at school and sings in the barn as practice because she's too loud in the house. She likes to climb up into the rafters and dream about flying. Edith refers to her brother and herself as "under-protected" because their father is never around. She has a pellet gun and practices shooting things as a form of protection. She likes French bread pizza. She spends a lot of time at home, by herself, watching old VHS tapes. She has a Rubik's cube.

She is aware of the fact that Kenny does everything for her, including buying her Christmas presents. She loves him a lot. She doesn't like adults.

Given Circumstances
Who are they? Edith is by herself, talking to her stuffed frog.

Where are they? She is sitting in the barn rafters.

When does this take place? Over the course of a few months in the early 1990s.

Why are they there? She is there singing and avoiding the harsh realities of her life.

What is the pre-beat? This monologue opens the play.

Questions
1. Can you state your objective in a simple, specific, and active way?
2. Whom are you talking to? Be specific and have a clear image. "The audience" isn't specific enough.
3. Can you think of three adjectives to describe your character?
4. Why do you like being high up in the air?
5. How did you climb into the rafters?

6. What songs do you sing up here?
7. What's the name of your stuffed frog?
8. Do you miss your mom?
9. What do you remember most about her?
10. How often do you talk to your dad?
11. What does he look like?
12. Is Kenny a good brother?
13. Is he a good mother/father/parent?
14. How often do you practice shooting?
15. How good are you at hitting your target?

Edith Can Shoot Things and Hit Them
A. Rey Pamatmat

EDITH

Do you know Mrs. Osheyack? Or Dina Osheyack? Her brother goes to your school.

I'm friends with Dina, and one time her mom drives me home from choir. And Dina's mom has to pee so bad, she comes in the house. I don't want her to, but she does.

And the house is a mess. She asks, "Is anyone here?" Dad is at work. Kenny is still at yearbook. She gets all weird about it. I show her how when I'm home I microwave food for dinner. Or, if I know Kenny is coming home fast, how I start the rice cooker. But it makes her even more upset, so she plants herself in the living room and waits till Kenny gets home. She even cleans the living room a little bit.

And then she keeps calling, for weeks after that, asking for my dad. And, finally, they talk. And then he yells at Kenny for not keeping the house clean, and then he yells at me for letting someone inside.

So Kenny doesn't really let anyone in the house anymore. And he cleans a lot.

Did Mrs. Osheyack hire you to spy on us?

Analysis: *Edith Can Shoot Things and Hit Them*

Type: Seriocomic
Synopsis

Edith and Kenny, her brother, live with their father on a remote piece of property far from town. There is a house, a barn, and an orchard. Edith has very few friends but a very vivid imagination. She sits in the eaves of the barn with a pellet gun and dreams of being a "big, grown-up girl."

Edith and Kenny have a rough relationship with their father. He's mostly absent, preferring to stay at his girlfriend's house. He forgets to put money in the bank that they need for food and gas. Kenny spends most of his free time at his friend Benji's house. The mother of one of Edith's friends will call from time to time to check in and make sure Edith is eating the right things. Edith, tired of being alone all the time, tells Kenny to make Benji come over to their house. This small event precipitates a lot of action: Benji kisses Kenny while Edith does homework in the other room; Kenny and Benji go into the barn and begin a sexual relationship since there are no adults around. Kenny finds the nerve to call his dad and demand money.

Kenny and Benji carry on their relationship as secretly as possible. Kenny doesn't want anyone to find out their dad isn't there, because then the state would split Edith and him apart. Benji's mom, however, finds out about the relationship and does not handle it well. Benji moves in with Edith and Kenny.

Edith hears a noise late one night and shoots the pellet gun out the window. She ends up hitting Chloe, her dad's girlfriend, who has to go to the hospital and have a pellet removed from her shoulder. As punishment, Edith's father sends her to a private Catholic reform school. She escapes, and Kenny once again threatens their father into letting Edith stay under Kenny's "custody."

Character Description

Edith, almost 13 years old

Edith is a Filipino-American whose mother has passed away, and she lives with her brother. She has a giant stuffed frog named Feigie. She is in choir at school and sings in the barn as practice because she's too loud in the house. She likes to climb up into the rafters and dream about flying. Edith refers to her brother and herself as "under-protected" because their father is never around. She has a pellet gun and practices shooting things as a form of protection. She likes French bread pizza. She spends a lot of time at home, by herself, watching old VHS tapes. She has a Rubik's cube.

She is aware of the fact that Kenny does everything for her, including buying her Christmas presents. She loves him a lot. She doesn't like adults.

Given Circumstances

Who are they? Benji is Kenny's best friend and, Edith suspects, something more.

Where are they? The living room of Edith's house.

When does this take place? Over the course of a few months in the early 1990s.

Why are they there? Edith lives here, Benji is visiting Kenny.

What is the pre-beat? Edith pulls a bow and arrow on Benji.

Questions

1. Can you state your objective in a simple, specific, and active way?
2. Who are you talking to? Be specific and have a clear image.
3. Can you think of three adjectives to describe your character?
4. Is Kenny a good brother/father/mother/parental figure to you?
5. Do you miss your mom?
6. How often do you speak to your dad?

7. When is the last time you saw your dad?
8. What does Benji look like?
9. What made you suspect there's something more than friendship happening between Kenny and Benji?
10. How often does Benji come over?
11. Do you like having him around?
12. What are your household chores?
13. Do you do them?
14. Is there any boy at school you like?
15. What's the urgency behind this monologue?

Playing with Grown Ups
Hannah Patterson

STELLA

I find adults fascinating. I could watch them, for hours. Much more than animals at the zoo. They make everything in life so complicated. Then they say, 'Uh, if only everything in life wasn't so complicated.' But I swear they enjoy it. They create it.

To me it all seems so simple. If you like someone, tell them. If someone is hurt, then help them. Sort out the problem, at the root. Don't just patch it up, or ignore it. It'll only come back, and it'll hurt more next time.

My mum always says to me 'You don't understand because you haven't experienced it yet. Once you experience it, then you'll know. Then you'll feel it. Then you'll be able to empathize. Life is complicated.'

She talks as if I were an innocent. A blank canvas. But I'm not. She's the one that's forgotten. We aren't born innocent. We're just born more obvious, that's all. With all our needs and desires right out there in front of us, naked, for everyone to see. And then we learn to hide them. Call them by different names. Make them seem more sophisticated. To complicate it.

Don't we?

Well, that's how I see it.

Analysis: *Playing with Grown Ups*

Type: Seriocomic
Synopsis

Joanna and Robert have just had a baby, Lily nine weeks ago. Robert works all day while Joanna is home with their daughter. Things are tense between the two as they try to juggle their new way of life. Joanna is tired all the time and trying to lose the baby weight; she also may be drinking more wine than she should.

Robert has run into their friend Jake and invited him over for dinner without asking Joanna. Joanna isn't dressed or prepared for company. She doesn't consider Jake her friend anymore. When Jake appears with the much younger Stella, Joanna throws Robert an "I told you so" look. The new parents try to act like everything is okay in the house. Joanna is also an academic whose field of study is women who've been written out of history, which is perhaps how she's feeling now that she's had a baby and put her professional life on hold.

As the evening goes on, Stella surprises everyone with how smart, intuitive, and probing her mind is. In a way, she's the most grown up of anyone there. Robert is jealous of Jake's relationship and condemning of it. Joanna continues to drink too much and forgets to turn the oven on for dinner.

Robert knows that his department is under financial strain. Jake's monologue drives home the fact that his job is at stake and he should perhaps be looking for another one. When Robert and Stella go to check on the crying baby, Jake tries to rekindle his old romance with Joanna. She admits she's made a terrible mistake.

Stella and Jake crash on the sofa, and Robert has a bit of a meltdown. The stress of everything is too much for him, and Jake gets the brunt of his anger. Lily starts crying, and Joanna makes Robert take her out of the apartment. Stella is the one who soothes everyone back into place.

Joanna finally admits that her career is more important to her than her family. The dead women she's trying to restore to the world mean more to her than the living child in the other room. She leaves.

Character Description
Stella, 16
Stella is dating the much older Jake. She loves babies and hopes to have lots of them eventually. She believes family is really the only thing that matters. She just finished reading Jane Austen's *Pride and Prejudice* and loved it. She knows very little about Jake, and the evening is a series of discoveries about what he does for a living and what he wants from life. She knows a lot about film and surprised Jake with her intense, probing questions at his lecture. Then she asked him out for a drink. She doesn't want to go to university.

Given Circumstances
Who are they? Stella is a sixteen-year-old girl.
Where are they? Joanna and Robert's apartment.
When does this take place? The present.
Why are they there? She is dating Jake, Joanna and Robert's best friend.
What is the pre-beat? This monologue opens the play.

Questions
1. Can you state your objective in a simple, specific, and active way?
2. Whom are you talking to? Be specific and have a clear image.
3. Can you think of three adjectives to describe your character?
4. How did Stella wind up at Jake's lecture?
5. What sparked her interest in cinema?
6. Does she often ask older men out?
7. When she asked him for a drink, was she pursuing him romantically?

8. What does she find attractive about Jake?

9. What does he look like?

10. How does he make her feel?

11. Has she dated older men before?

12. When did she tell him that she was saving her virginity until she was in love?

13. Does her mother approve of the relationship?

14. She never mentions her father. Where is he?

15. How would she define a "grownup"?

Lessons from an Abandoned Work
Mona Pirnot

KHAYA

If I wasn't afraid of anything? Geez, I don't know, Fiona. You want the violins to underscore me being like "I would pursue my dreams." Like in the movies when a steel-welder should be a dancer. But, honestly, I do what I want. Like I just said, I don't know that my fear holds me back from living life.

I mean, I guess if I had to say one thing, let me think . . . you're putting me on the spot here.

Hmm. I guess I'm afraid of commitment. Which, I think, is something I'll grow out of and I don't know that I would have it any other way right now. But I do want to settle down some day. Have a husband and kids. But the thought of being with just one person right now, kinda freaks me out. In twenty years, I don't want to find myself really far gone into a committed relationship and thinking "I wish I would have tasted every flavor in the ice cream shop before promising to eat Rocky Road forever and having marshmallows stuck in my teeth for the rest of my life."

Okay, that was a really bad extended metaphor.

Analysis: *Lessons from an Abandoned Work*

Type: Seriocomic
Synopsis
"There is no 'right time' to work through the bullshit in your life. Don't abandon your work midstream when things get hard."

Fiona is having trouble relating to the world. Most of her college teachers spout generic concepts without probing the real depths of the issues at hand. Her fellow, overprivileged students parrot their parents or the news headlines they read on the Internet. Fiona wants more. She volunteers at an assisted living facility for the elderly where she has befriended Arnaud, a stylish ninety-year-old Frenchman. They read Beckett's *Waiting for Godot* out loud to each other, and Arnaud probes Fiona about her life and pushes her to realize her true self, because he never got to be the best, most honest version of himself. Fiona feels closer to Arnaud than almost anyone else in her life, and as a gift to him, she enrolls in a playwriting class to write a documentary-style piece that questions what people are afraid of in their lives. Nate is the only other student enrolled in the class.

Fiona's parents expect her to pursue a career in politics in Washington, D.C. When they find out that Fiona is thinking about adding a theater arts minor, they threaten to kick her out of the house and cut off her tuition payments. Fiona moves out and into the dorm room of her best/only friend, Khaya.

Khaya, the polar opposite of Fiona, is more adventurous, more sexually open, and more savvy. She comes up with the idea of Fiona writing papers for students in order to make tuition money. Arnaud finds out about this, and he and Fiona have a fight. She says things to him that she deeply regrets. She has sex with Nate. The school discovers her deceit and suspends her. Khaya discovers she's pregnant. Nate offers no comfort. Arnaud dies, but he and Fiona make peace.

Edie, Fiona's playwriting teacher, is the one person who manages to motivate Fiona into getting back into the world. Fiona manages to reinstate herself into the school, and she changes her major to playwriting.

Character Description
Khaya, late teens

Fiona's best friend. Sometimes she seems distracted, and it might be because she's more concerned with her next sexual conquest than she is with her schoolwork. Khaya lets Fiona stay with her on the condition that Fiona write a one-page, double-spaced paper for economics class and stay out of the apartment every night from 9:00 to 11:00 p.m.

Khaya thinks Fiona needs to have more fun and challenges her to work through her many ingrained fears.

Khaya also gets suspended for Fiona's paper-writing scheme, and instead of accepting any of the blame, she puts it all on Fiona. She also discovers that she's pregnant and kicks Fiona out of the apartment.

Given Circumstances
Who are they? Fiona is Khaya's best friend.
Where are they? Khaya's dorm room.
When does this take place? The present.
Why are they there? Fiona is crashing with Khaya while she figures her life out.
What is the pre-beat? Fiona is writing a play and asked Khaya what she would do if she wasn't afraid of anything.

Questions
1. Can you state your objective in a simple, specific, and active way?
2. Whom are you talking to? Be specific and have a clear image.
3. Can you think of three adjectives to describe your character?
4. How long have you and Fiona been friends?
5. Why do you think you get along so well?
6. How long has she been staying with you?
7. You have a (different) guy over every night, and Fiona interrupted tonight. Are you mad at her?

8. What are you opinions about Fiona being a virgin?

9. Fiona kissed her first boy tonight. Are you proud of her?

10. What's your major?

11. Are you a good student?

12. What do you plan on doing when you graduate?

13. Have you ever been with a guy thinking "he's the one"?

14. How would you define commitment?

15. What's the urgency behind this monologue?

Lessons from an Abandoned Work
Mona Pirnot

FIONA

Okay.

God, how do I get this from here (*touches her head*) to there? (*gestures outside of herself*)

Well . . . sometimes . . . I have out of body experiences.

No. C'mon. I don't mean any of this to be taken literally. Sometimes I just get too "in-my-head." That's the best way to describe it. I shrink down inside myself and become an observer who is incapable of functioning alongside the actors. You know what I mean by actors? Not like stage actors. Just "actors" as in people who have no problem fitting in. They're all cast in their parts. They all know what to do. And then there's me. I just watch and I have no idea what the fuck everybody is talking about.

And this isn't how I am all the time or anything but I'll get into certain situations where, like, people are being too civilized or taking themselves too seriously or doing some shit that I can't go along with and instead of catching on, I get totally left behind. People are puppets and I get sweaty. . . .

Oh God. I told you you didn't want to know.

Analysis: *Lessons from an Abandoned Work*

Type: Seriocomic
Synopsis

"There is no 'right time' to work through the bullshit in your life. Don't abandon your work midstream when things get hard."

Fiona is having trouble relating to the world. Most of her college teachers spout generic concepts without probing the real depths of the issues at hand. Her fellow, overprivileged students parrot their parents or the news headlines they read on the Internet. Fiona wants more.

She volunteers at an assisted living facility for the elderly where she has befriended Arnaud, a stylish ninety-year-old Frenchman. They read Beckett's *Waiting for Godot* out loud to each other, and Arnaud probes Fiona about her life and pushes her to realize her true self, because he never got to be the best, most honest version of himself. Fiona feels closer to Arnaud than almost anyone else in her life, and as a gift to him, she enrolls in a playwriting class to write a documentary-style piece that questions what people are afraid of in their lives. Nate is the only other student enrolled in the class.

Fiona's parents expect her to pursue a career in politics in Washington, D.C. When they find out that Fiona is thinking about adding a theater arts minor, they threaten to kick her out of the house and cut off her tuition payments. Fiona moves out and into the dorm room of her best/only friend, Khaya.

Khaya, the polar opposite of Fiona, is more adventurous, more sexually open, and more savvy. She comes up with the idea of Fiona writing papers for students in order to make tuition money. Arnaud finds out about this, and he and Fiona have a fight. She says things to him that she deeply regrets. She has sex with Nate. The school discovers her deceit and suspends her. Khaya discovers she's pregnant. Nate offers no comfort. Arnaud dies, but he and Fiona make peace.

Edie, Fiona's playwriting teacher, is the one person who manages to motivate Fiona into getting back into the world. Fiona manages to reinstate herself into the school, and she changes her major to playwriting.

Character Description
Fiona, late teens
Eager, zealous, and driven—often to the edge of her sanity. She wants to live in a better world, a world in which her teachers are better and her peers learn to formulate their own opinions. She also can't seem to communicate with her parents, who despite their good intentions don't really know or understand their daughter. They think her happiness/success will come from a political life. Fiona can't even smile naturally on cue.

Fiona is a triple major in political science, journalism, and international studies and wants to add a playwriting minor to that course load.

She has a deep, loving relationship with Arnaud, and so she drops her international studies major in order to pick up the playwriting minor. She leaves home to pursue this, saying, "I do not have to do everything my parents want me to."

She's a virgin who has never really had a real romantic relationship because she's too busy with schoolwork. She lets Nate kiss her but then leaves because she's scared.

Given Circumstances
Who are they? Nate and Fiona are classmates and potential love interests.
Where are they? Nate has taken Fiona on a walk on campus.
When does this take place? The present.

Why are they there? They've had an intense class, and Nate wants to show Fiona his secret spot.

What is the pre-beat? Nate told Fiona he was watching her in class and wondered what was going in her mind.

Questions

1. Can you state your objective in a simple, specific, and active way?
2. Whom are you talking to? Be specific and have a clear image.
3. Can you think of three adjectives to describe your character?
4. What do you find most attractive about Nate?
5. Does he make your nervous? Happy? Scared?
6. Why haven't you had a boyfriend yet?
7. Has a boy ever asked you out before?
8. What has your relationship with Arnaud done for your self-confidence?
9. What is it about writing that you find attractive?
10. Do you write every day?
11. Do you share your writing with anyone?
12. What does it feel like to be "in your head" all the time?
13. Do you have any tricks for getting out of your head?
14. You call yourself "offputting." How so?
15. What's the urgency behind this monologue?

A Numbers Game
Tanya Saracho

ONE

My boyfriend, he doesn't know what to do with me, because even though he tells me that I look fine to him, fine is not enough to me. Do you know what fine means? Fine means, I'll fucking tolerate you. That's what fine means.

Fine means, "Sure, but could we please turn the lights off so I don't have to look at you?" Fine means "Our days are counted, baby, unless you do something about your weight." Fine is people looking at you when you put anything in your mouth because all of a sudden you've turned into a social pariah. I sat there yesterday at a restaurant, and these two assholes were having some kind of a ball over at their table as I was trying to eat my freakin' lunch.

The two actually sat there staring at me, as I put the sandwich in my mouth. It was so embarrassing. I'm sitting there alone, which I hate in the first place, and these two douchebags are like whispering something—I notice cuz they're giggling like little girls over there. So I look and they don't really stop.

I try to ignore them but I mean, I have to freakin' eat my food, right? I have 45 minutes for lunch, I have to eat this thing. And I can feel their freakin' eyes on me, like burning across the restaurant and I say fuck it and take another bite and they . . . These two jerks makes this noise. Like . . .

(*Beat.*)

And I know what that noise is. I know what it means.

How did I let it get this bad?

Analysis: *A Numbers Game*

Type: Dramatic
Synopsis and Character Description

This monologue comes from a very short play that was part of Humana Festival's 2012 collection of plays and monologues centered around food and its complexities, performed under the title *Oh, Gastronomy!*

Two females (One and Two) and one male (Three) speak directly to the audience. They are aware of one another, but they do not interact. One holds a bag of marbles in her hand and has a fishbowl in front of her. Every time she says a number, she drops a marble in the bowl.

The marbles correspond with gaining weight, each marble equaling a pound. One says the first goes unnoticed. In fact, the first five can go undetected. It could be water weight making the scale go up a little every day. It's not until you gain seven or eight pounds that it really becomes apparent. And then when people start to comment on it is when it's really a problem.

Your face starts to look different. You begin to feel different. Then you gain fifteen pounds and you have to buy new pants. One tries a cleanse diet involving cayenne pepper. It doesn't work. One tries Zumba and other fitness trends, but the weight still keeps coming. She feels like she's gaining weight by just breathing. One begins to move differently. She begins to wear more sweatshirts. She doesn't recognize herself in the mirror. Suddenly she's gained thirty pounds and she doesn't want to have sex because she feels ugly.

One feels like she's had no control over this situation.

Given Circumstances

Who are they? One is talking to the audience.
Where are they? She could be anywhere, it's up to you.
When does this take place? The present.

Why are they there? She's dealing with weight issues.

What is the pre-beat? She's just recounted her weight gain and feels disgusted by it.

Questions

1. Can you state your objective in a simple, specific, and active way?
2. Whom are you talking to? Be specific and have a clear image.
3. Can you think of three adjectives to describe your character?
4. "The audience" isn't specific enough. Whom could you be speaking to?
5. Where could this conversation be taking place?
6. You've put on almost thirty pounds. How?
7. What are all the things in your life that make you unhappy so that you turn to food?
8. What does your boyfriend look like?
9. How long have you two been together?
10. Is he overweight? In shape?
11. How do *you* feel about your body?
12. Have you gained weight before, or is the first time?
13. How has it affected other facets of your life?
14. How many diets have you been on? Which ones?
15. Do you think you can actually fix the problem?

Port
Simon Stephens

RACHEAL

Nana. I'm going to get a flat. Up Edgely. I'm dead excited.
I am. It's really smart. It's got a bathroom. Kitchen. Got a
shower. It's cracking. Rent's thirty quid a week. I can afford that.
It's all right.

Nana. I need some money. For the deposit. I need two hundred and forty pound. For the deposit, which is a month's rent,
and for a month's rent in advance. Nana I've not got it. I can't
afford the deposit. I was going to ask you. If you had it. If I could
borrow it from you. If you could lend it to us.

Can you Nana? Can you lend us the deposit? The two hundred
and forty pound?

Nana? Did you hear what I said? I've not got it. If I don't get
the deposit and the rent then I'll lose the flat. I'll pay you back.
I will Nana, I swear. On my life. I'll pay you back. Every month.
I could pay you like twenty quid a month or summit. I could do
that. I could afford that. Nana. On my life.

I thought, Mum always said you were . . . didn't Grand-dad
leave you any? Didn't Grand-dad, I thought—Grand-dad always
said there was money . . .

He always said, he told me, Grand-dad told me there was some
money and if that, if I ever needed some money badly that he
would find it for me and he would lend it to me. He told me. He
promised.

Analysis: *Port*

Type: Dramatic
Synopsis and Character Description

The play follows the life of Racheal Keats from the age of eleven to the age of twenty-four. She lives in Stockport, Greater Manchester, England. One actress plays Racheal throughout the course of the play.

In the first scene Racheal, her mother (Christine), and her younger brother (Billy) are sitting in a car staring at their apartment. Billy, in typical younger-brother mode, is kicking the back of Racheal's seat. They are out there because Racheal's dad has locked the door and shut off all the lights, and is sitting in the apartment by himself. There is something wrong with him. Racheal think he's weird and that he hates them.

Racheal tells her mother the first memory she has is of finding a dead sparrow in their yard and wrapping it in a paper tissue. She also remembers that when she was little, her mother would put the kids in her bed for warmth and call Racheal her hot water bottle. She wants to be glamorous and wear makeup when she grows up. Racheal is scared of her father. She's desperately trying to make a connection to her mother, but Christine isn't listening.

In the following scene, a few years later, Racheal sits in a hospital waiting room. Her grandfather is sick. Her mother has left without a word. He dad comes in and tells her that her granddad has died. Rachael blames her dad for the death, saying he broke her grandfather's heart because of the way he treated Christine. The problem is, Racheal is growing up and there's no one around to properly guide or protect her. The older Racheal gets, the more she wants to get out of this small town, but she doesn't know how. Ever since her grandfather died, she's scared of death. Billy is getting out of control from lack of discipline.

Racheal gets a job at a supermarket. She has a failed marriage. She has an affair. She spends her whole life worrying about Billy. In the end she decides the only thing she can do is leave town.

Given Circumstances

Who are they? Anne is Racheal's seventy-four-year-old, blind grandmother.

Where are they? The garden of Anne's nursing home.

When does this take place? 1994.

Why are they there? Racheal has come to ask for a loan.

What is the pre-beat? Racheal has just described the apartment and the low rent.

Questions

1. Can you state your objective in a simple, specific, and active way?
2. Whom are you talking to? Be specific and have a clear image.
3. Can you think of three adjectives to describe your character?
4. Are you close to your grandmother?
5. How often do you visit her?
6. Does she look like your mother?
7. How badly do you need/want this apartment?
8. Are you living at home with your dad and brother?
9. How long has it been since your mom left?
10. What's it like not knowing where she went or when you'll speak to her again?
11. What do you miss most about your grandfather?
12. When did he tell you that you could have this money?
13. Was your expectation that your grandmother would just give you the money?

14. Where were your grandparents when things were rough with your father?

15. How much money do you make at the supermarket?

Ancient Gods of the Backwoods
Kathryn Walat

JACKIE

I missed class tonight—didn't even get to shower—and I'm *pissed* because it was going to be a good one: dysfunctional families—I *know* that—I could have shared.

In my version of this story—my ideal: tits, out to here—no, why did I—that's not *my*. I'm like: no tits at all. Like those Olympic athletes—wings on their feet—the ones who *run* and run and run and don't even get their periods. Convenient: they can't get pregnant, at least not in high school, which is the trick around these—scratch that. Stupid. Stupid.

But I'm not stupid. I've just been. Dealing with. Tragic events. Mom hung herself behind the bar when I was 12, when she figured out my dad—that he was actually her—all that was not *nice*. The gods saw it coming—didn't stop it—how could they let that *happen*? But I'm saving that for psych class: dysfunctional families. So. Me. This is. Me. Me. Me.

I've got something inside of me that I wish wasn't there. And I know I'm not alone here. Right? America the beautiful. I think that if I could only. If I were living a normal, happy, normal life, maybe it would go away. You might call it *rage*. But that sounds too—

And it's ordinary—you could walk into any supermarket or liquor store in any town and find it. There. The guy standing at the register next to the beef jerky: him or her or him—hitting the buttons on the lotto machine—or her. Me. You.

Most of the time, things are OK. But then something stupid will happen and it all falls apart and you think: really? I mean: really? You think: *really*, this is really how it—*is*?

Analysis: *Ancient Gods of the Backwoods*

Type: Seriocomic
Synopsis

The action of the play takes place in a land that's off the beaten track. It's not pretty and it's rural; a place the god's don't give a shit about. Just because the gods have forgotten about these people doesn't mean that they're don't exist. The town even has an oracle, even if it's covered with beer cans and graffiti.

It's hunting season, and the men went out to the woods the previous weekend—not all of them came back. Anne's two brothers died while hunting. Her mother, who owned the bar, hanged herself. Anne's father blinded himself. Walat references Greek mythology not only in the title, but in the action of the play. This story is an attempt by Anne to take control of her entire life, on an epic scale. Her family seems to be "tragically fucked." She's trying to figure out if she needs to be, as well.

Anne tries to have sex with Damon, her boyfriend, in the forest, but he says the time isn't right. She always wants to do things when she's ready. He works at Karl's bar and has to get to work, so there probably isn't enough time. Damon dreams of opening a landscaping business.

Karl is getting the bar in order. Although maintaining the business is important, it's the illegal numbers game that happens in the bar that's more important.

Anne thinks the deer that Karl shot is calling to her for a proper burial. She wants Jackie to help her bury it before Karl hangs its head in the bar. Jackie won't help her, so Anne steals the deer, cuts off its antlers, and buries it—but not very deep. Karl is furious. She says the gods made her do it. Karl tells Damon he has to punish Anne for her betrayal.

Walat is exploring the idea of free will versus destiny: how much of our lives is really in our control.

Jackie, knowing that Karl is going to go after Anne, comes in to the bar with a shotgun, and instead of being a chicken shit, she shoots and kills him. Then she turns to Anne for guidance, because Anne is the one who always knows what to do.

Character Description
Jackie, late teens

Jackie works at the A&P and goes to school at night. She's the older sister of Anne. Her brothers, both of whom are now dead, were not very nice men. At work she has to wear a uniform that is snug around her somewhat ample chest. She had better not catch you looking at it. Jackie likes Big Red gum, and she likes to talk about things she knows to a willing audience. Jackie likes power. She also believes in Artemis, goddess of hunting. Her mom used to give her quarters to play Patsy Cline on the jukebox. She always wished they had been a normal family.

Given Circumstances

Who are they? Jackie is talking to the audience.

Where are they? Off the beaten track, rural, a place the gods don't give a shit about.

When does this take place? The present, during hunting season.

Why are they there? This is where Jackie lives, works, and goes to school.

What is the pre-beat? This speech begins the scene.

Questions

1. Can you state your objective in a simple, specific, and active way?
2. Whom are you talking to? Be specific and have a clear image.
3. Can you think of three adjectives to describe your character?
4. "The audience" isn't specific enough, so who else could you be speaking to?
5. What's small town life like?
6. The allusions in this play are all of very epic proportions. How is your need/want/desire epic?
7. What is it like working in the A&P?
8. What's your job there?
9. When do you go to school?
10. What are you studying?
11. Do you plan on leaving town one day?
12. How has the dysfunction of your family influenced/affected you?
13. Do you have a relationship to religion or the gods?
14. How would you define a "normal" family?
15. Have you ever killed or thought about killing a person before?

Exit Exam
Mara Wilson

SARA MICHELLE

OK, everyone laughs when I tell them this, but my hero is Pat Benatar.

It's not because of her skills as a singer—I mean, I do like her voice, but I'm not like a superfan, I actually only have her Greatest Hits. It's more because of the image of the person I have created from her music.

My ex-boyfriend Robin once told me about "concept albums," which are albums where all the songs are connected in a story or theme. To me, Pat Benatar is, like, a "concept singer" because all of her albums and songs sort of connect in a way that tells a story of a person, and I can really relate to that person. For example, a lot of her earlier music is about how she was always a nice girl, always good and everything, but then she changed. But it wasn't her fault—she didn't *decide* to be a bad girl, but someone used her in a way that forced her to become one. I think that's what "Heartbreaker" is about: it's like she's saying, "Look what you did to me!" And I can relate to that feeling a lot because I was a good girl once, too.

But anyway, in her later albums she becomes stronger and overcomes her helplessness. At least I think those songs are on her later albums—I mean, I only have her Greatest Hits. Anyway, she got stronger and learned that she could love and be loved, and that gives me hope for myself. When I'm feeling upset I can listen to "Promises in the Dark" and know that someone else has been there before. Oh, and right before I had to break up with Bradley I listened to "Treat Me Right" and I knew I was doing the right thing and that I deserved better. And then before I actually did it I listened to "Hit Me With Your Best Shot" because it always makes me feel powerful. So, as you can see, Pat Benatar is my hero and a guiding light for me.

I mean, unless she doesn't write her own songs. Then my hero's probably my mom.

Analysis: *Exit Exam*

Type: Seriocomic
Synopsis and Character Description
This piece was written as a stand-alone monologue, so all of the factual information you need about the character and events can be found within.

Exit exams are tests that many American students need to pass in order to graduate from high school. That would put Sara Michelle anywhere between the ages of sixteen and nineteen. First you need to decide how someone born in the late 1990s has become familiar with the work of a female pop star who reached the pinnacle of her career in the mid- to late 1980s. At the end of the monologue, Sara Michelle mentions her mother as a possible hero and it could be that she is the one who, knowingly or unknowingly, introduced her daughter to the music icon.

The idea of a concept album seems to be what Sara Michelle appreciates most in this scenario, and perhaps it's because she looks at herself as a concept. It would appear that Sara Michelle also started out as a good girl, the one who did everything right, who could be depended upon in any situation, who was responsible and achieved good grades. And maybe now she's not so good. Perhaps circumstances in her own life are leading her to change for the worse.

She mentions having had two boyfriends, Robin and Bradley, but tells us very little about them. However, talking about "Promises in the Dark" and "Treat Me Right" lets us know that these boys didn't treat her all that well. Or said they were going to do one thing and then acted another way. "Heartbreaker" lets us know that Sara Michelle has found her heart broken at least once.

There's no mention of Sara Michelle's father. Is Sara Michelle repeating patterns in relationships she's learned from her mother? She talks about wanting/deserving to be loved. It seems like her mother loves her. He friends probably love her. She's looking for a deeper, more intimate love, but as a work-in-progress she might not be quite ready for it yet.

Be careful when performing this monologue that you don't fall into portraying Sara Michelle as a victim. Her love of Pat Benatar means that she's trying to emulate her in some way, and so Sara Michelle probably presents a tough facade. She has a big heart underneath, though, and has probably opened it up one or two times. I do not get the feeling from this piece that Sara Michelle is giving up. Rather, it seems to me that she's digging deep to find her strength and define what she needs and who she wants to be.

Given Circumstances

Who are they? Sara Michelle is talking to the audience.
Where are they? She could be in her room or at school.
When does this take place? The present.
Why are they there? She has to answer this question and pass in order to graduate.

What is the pre-beat? Someone has asked her to speak/write on who her hero is.

Questions

1. Can you state your objective in a simple, specific, and active way?
2. Who are you talking to? Be specific and have a clear image.
3. Can you think of three adjectives to describe your character?
4. Who is Pat Benatar?
5. How did you discover her?
6. What's your favorite song by her?
7. What does she look like now? When she was at the height of her fame?
8. "The audience" isn't specific enough; who in particular could you be speaking to?
9. Do you have any other heroes?
10. Are your mom or your dad your hero?
11. How long did you think about the question?
12. Have you had to take any other exit exams?
13. In what ways were you a good girl?
14. How are you a bad girl now?
15. What event happened in your life to make you change?

ACKNOWLEDGMENTS

To all my teachers and mentors—there are almost too many to name—who had a hand in shaping my view on theater and how I teach it: Helen White, Jim Carnahan, Nicky Martin, Rob Marshall, Sam Mendes, John Crowley, David Leveaux, Susan Bristow, and Amy Saltz.

To the people who read and advised on initial drafts of the book: Dennis Flanagan, David A. Miller, and Saidah Arrika Ekulona.

To Katya Campbell for introducing me to more playwrights that the world needs to know.

To all the playwrights and agents represented here, for their permission.

To Mom, Dad, and Joe.

PLAY SOURCES AND ACKNOWLEDGMENTS

should be addressed to Derek Zasky, WME, 1325 Avenue of the
Americas, New York, NY 10019.

Ancient Gods of the Backwoods by Kathryn Walat. Copyright 2014 by
Kathryn Walat. Used by permission of Kathryn Walat. All inquiries
should be addressed to Seth Glewen, Gersh Agency, 41 Madison
Avenue, 33rd Floor, New York, NY 10010.

Apocalypse Apartment by Allison Moore. Copyright 2014 by Allison
Moore. Used by permission of Allison Moore. All inquiries should
be addressed to Chris Till, Creative Artists Agency, 405 Lexington
Avenue, 19th Floor, New York, NY 10174.

Appropriate by Branden Jacobs-Jenkins. Copyright 2014 by Branden
Jacobs-Jenkins. Used by permission of Branden Jacobs-Jenkins. All
inquiries should be addressed to Derek Zasky, WME, 1325 Avenue of
the Americas, New York, NY 10019.

Baby Girl by Edith Freni. Copyright 2006 by Edith Freni. Used by
permission of Edith Freni. All inquiries should be addressed to Ron
Gwiazda, Abrams Artists Agency, 275 7th Avenue, 26th Floor, New
York, NY 10001.

Burnt Orange by Lila Feinberg. Copyright 2011 by Lila Feinberg.
Used by permission of Ron West. All inquiries should be addressed
to Ron West at Thruline Entertainment, west@thrulinela.com/
westasst@thrulinela.com.

Chronicles Simpkins Will Cut Your Ass by Rolin Jones. Copyright
2008 by Rolin Jones. Used by permission of Chris Till. All inquiries

should be addressed to Chris Till, Creative Artists Agency, 405 Lexington Avenue, 19th Floor, New York, NY 10174.

Cutting by Kathleen Germann. Copyright 2014 by Kathleen Germann. Used by permission of Kathleen Germann. All inquiries should be addressed to the playwright at Kathlngrmnn@gmail.com.

Dig Dig Dig by Nikole Beckwith. Copyright 2011 by Nikole Beckwith. Used by permission of Nikole Beckwith. All inquiries should be addressed to Oliver Sultan, Creative Artists Agency, 405 Lexington Avenue, 19th Floor, New York, NY 10174.

Don't Talk, Don't See by Julie Jensen. Copyright 2014 by Julie Jensen. Used by permission of Susan Gurman. All inquiries should be addressed to The Susan Gurman Agency, LLC, 1501 Broadway, 30th Floor, New York, NY 10036, susan@gurmanagency.com.

Edith Can Shoot Things and Hit Them by A. Rey Pamatmat. Copyright 2012 by A. Rey Pamatmat. Used by permission of A. Rey Pamatmat. All inquiries should be addressed to Beth Blickers, Abrams Artists Agency, 275 7th Avenue, 26th Floor, New York, NY 10001, beth.blickers@abramsartny.com.

Exit Exam by Mara Wilson. Copyright 2008 by Maria Wilson. Used by permission of Maria Wilson. All inquiries should be addressed to Alyssa Reuben, Paradigm Agency, 360 Park Avenue South, 16th Floor, New York, NY 10010, or to the author at MariaWilsonwritesstuff.com.

Four from *Where Do We Live and Other Plays* by Christopher Shinn. Copyright 1998, 2005. Used by permission of Theatre Communications Group. Inquiries should be addressed to Theatre Communications Group, 520 8th Avenue, 24th Floor, New York, NY, 10018

Franny's Way by Richard Nelson. Copyright 2003 by Richard Nelson. Used by permission of ICM Partners. All inquiries should be addressed to ICM Partners, 730 Fifth Avenue, 4th Floor, New York, NY 10019.

girl. by Megan Mostyn-Brown. Copyright 2002, 2008 by Megan Mostyn-Brown. Used by permission of Megan Mostyn-Brown. All inquiries should be addressed to Rachel Viola, United Talent Agency, 888 Seventh Avenue, 9th Floor, New York, NY 10106. Violar@unitedtalent.com.

Great Falls by Lee Blessing. Copyright 2009 by Lee Blessing. Used by permission All inquiries should be addressed to Judy Boals, Inc, 307 W. 38th Street, New York, NY 10018. judy@judyboals.com.

Henry's Law by Stacie Lents. Copyright 2014 by Stacie Lents. All rights reserved. Reprinted by permission of Playscripts, Inc. To purchase acting editions of this play, or to obtain stock and amateur performance rights, you must contact Playscripts, Inc. www.playscripts.co; email: info@playscripts.com; phone: 1-866-NEW-PLAY (639-7529). All other inquiries should be addressed to Amy Wagner, Abrams Artists Agebcy, 275 Seventh Avenue, 26th Floor, New York, NY 10001; email: Amy.Wagner@abramsartny.com; phone: 646-486-4600.

How We Got On by Idris Goodwin. Copyright 2013 by Idris Goodwin. All rights reserved. Reprinted by permission of Playscripts, Inc. To purchase acting editions of this play, or to obtain stock and

addressed to Permissions Manager, Bloomsbury Publishing, PLC 50 Bedford Square London, WC1B 3DP; contact@bloomsbury.com.

The Day I Stood Still by Kevin Elyot. Copyright 1998 by Kevin Elyot. Used by permission of Nick Hern Books. All inquiries should be addressed to Performing Rights Manager, Nick Hern Books, The Glasshouse, 49a Goldhawk Road, London, W12 8QP or info@ nickhernbooks.co.uk.

The Greatest Show on Earth by Michael Kimmel. Copyright 2014 by Michael Kimmel. Used by permission All inquiries should be addressed to Ron Gwiazda, Abrams Artists Agency, 275 7th Avenue, 26th Floor, New York, NY 10001.

The Tutor by Allan Havis. Copyright 2007 by Allan Havis. Used by permission of Susan Schulman. All inquiries should be addressed to the Susan Schulman Literary Agency, 454 West 44th Street, New York, NY 10036. schulman@aol.com.

Unlikely Jihadist by Michael Kimmel. Copyright 2014 by Michael Kimmel. Used by permission All inquiries should be addressed to Ron Gwiazda, Abrams Artists Agency, 275 7th Avenue, 26th Floor, New York, NY 10001

Untitled Matriarch Play (Or Seven Sisters) by Nikole Beckwith. Copyright 2013 by Nikole Beckwith. Used by permission of Nikole Beckwith. All inquiries should be addressed to Oliver Sultan, Creative Artists Agency, 405 Lexington Avenue, 19th Floor, New York, NY 10174.

Other Monologue and Scene Books